BAD NEWS FOR REFUGEES

Bad News for Refugees

Greg Philo,
Emma Briant
and Pauline Donald

PlutoPress
www.plutobooks.com

First published 2013 by Pluto Press
345 Archway Road, London N6 5AA

www.plutobooks.com

Distributed in the United States of America exclusively by
Palgrave Macmillan, a division of St. Martin's Press LLC,
175 Fifth Avenue, New York, NY 10010

British Library Cataloguing in Publication Data
A catalogue record for this book is available from the British Library

ISBN 978 0 7453 3433 2 Hardback
ISBN 978 0 7453 3432 5 Paperback
ISBN 978 1 8496 4957 5 PDF eBook
ISBN 978 1 8496 4959 9 Kindle eBook
ISBN 978 1 8496 4958 2 EPUB eBook

Library of Congress Cataloging in Publication Data applied for

This book is printed on paper suitable for recycling and made from fully managed
and sustained forest sources. Logging, pulping and manufacturing processes are
expected to conform to the environmental standards of the country of origin.

10 9 8 7 6 5 4 3 2 1

Typeset from disk by Curran Publishing Services, Norwich
Simultaneously printed digitally by CPI Antony Rowe, Chippenham, UK and
Edwards Bros in the United States of America

Contents

CONTENTS

Acknowledgements

Firstly we would like to thank all the asylum seekers and refugees, and their representatives and support workers, who kindly agreed to be interviewed for this book. Thanks also to the research team who helped in the gathering of data, Daniela Latina, Colin MacPherson, Catherine Happer and Mike Berry. We would also like to thank John Eldridge and David Miller of the Glasgow Media Group who helped us and gave us advice and encouragement. Thanks especially to Adrian Thomas, Anita Dullard, Katie Goodwin and the British Red Cross for their help and support, and to Dr Scott Blinder at the Oxford Migration Observatory. We would like to thank others in the Department of Sociology at Glasgow University: Giuliana Tiripelli, Chen Li and Yue Li. Thank you to Yajun Deng, Yasmin, Asad Muhammed and Rimshah Kausar, and Elisa Luo for helping us to set up the focus groups. John Mark Philo helped in this and also along with Anne Beach did a wonderful job with the editing, and may soon be working on the Latin translation.

Thank you also to all the journalists who spoke with us or offered us advice, and to Robert Webb and other members of the editorial and production team at Pluto Press. Pauline would like also to thank Dr Vassiliki Kolocotroni and Professor Richard Majors for their support. She would especially like to thank her family and friends who consistently encouraged and inspired her, Margaret Donald, Thomas Donald Senior, June Donald, Catherine Donald, Thomas Donald Junior, William Donald, Lynda-Anne Donald, David Donald, John Oguchukwu, Tony Vaughn and Carrie Jo Robinson. She offers love and thanks to her teacher El-Hajj Malik El-Shabazz. Finally thanks again to all those people who invested time, energy and enthusiasm in the research and production of the book.

Greg Philo, Emma Briant and Pauline Donald

Introduction

This book examines the media coverage of refugees and asylum seekers in the United Kingdom, and the impact this has on public understanding and on the everyday lives of different communities in Britain. Much of this coverage presents the issues of refuge and asylum as critical problems for the United Kingdom. Here we look at what the public is told and consider what is left out of the media narratives. We show how the TV and press coverage corresponds with key political events, and how politicians respond to public fears and anxieties which are themselves featured in and also generated by the popular press and other media.

We begin by introducing a short overview of the range of existing research in this area. This includes a brief history of how asylum and refuge have come to be major political issues of debate since the late 1990s. Our own research on the content of the British media follows. In this we analyse two key periods of media coverage in 2006 and 2011. The last section of this work includes a series of interviews with a range of people who have expert knowledge of the creation of media accounts. We also interviewed individuals who had direct experience of the impact media output has on people who are actually seeking asylum. These individuals included both refugees and those who work with them. Finally, we interviewed UK citizens from established migrant communities, who commented on the nature of media coverage and the impact that it had on their own lives.

Other Research

Most sociological studies have focused on 'race' or migration rather than asylum. This research has indicated that media representation of 'race', migration, refugees and asylum seekers largely presents these negatively as a source of 'moral panic', 'conflict', 'crisis' and 'threat'. The long-term trend in media coverage is to 'scapegoat', 'stereotype' and 'criminalise' migrant groups (Buchanan, Grillo and Threadgold, 2003; Castles and Kossack, 1973; Cohen, 2011; Finney, 2003; Hall

1

et al., 1978; Hartman and Husband, 1974; Kendall and Wolf, 1949; Philo and Beattie, 1999; Philo et al., 1998; Said, 1978; Van Diijk, 1991; Welch and Schuster, 2005).

A key phenomenon raised by media analysis in this area is the language used to describe contested issues. Since 2002, for example, attention has turned to the use of terms like 'illegal immigrant' in relation to those seeking asylum. Underpinning this terminology is the assumption that most asylum seekers are not in fact 'genuine' and that their motives are economic, something Alia and Bull refer to as the 'ineligibility myth' (2005: 27). The phrase 'illegal immigrant', imbued with the wholly negative connotations of 'illegality', conflates issues of refuge and asylum with economic immigration. In fact, most immigration and asylum laws are civil laws and not criminal laws; 'illegal', however, implies criminality. Asylum seekers have done nothing wrong. In 2003 the National Union of Journalists (NUJ) issued guidelines stating that:

> NO-ONE is an 'illegal asylum-seeker'. This term is always incorrect. It cannot be illegal to seek asylum since everyone has the fundamental human right to request asylum under international law.
>
> (NUJ, 2005)

Guidance for journalists produced by Oxfam, the National Union of Journalists, Amnesty International Scotland and the Scottish Refugee Council states that the phrase 'illegal immigrant':

> although commonly used, is not defined anywhere within UK law. The phrase 'illegal immigrant' was found in January 2002 by the Advertising Standards Authority to be racist, offensive and misleading.
>
> (NUJ, 2005: 14)

The term 'illegal immigrant' inhibits an informed debate over the issues at stake, as it does not distinguish between categories of migrant. There is also a tendency for asylum seekers whose applications have failed to be considered illegal immigrants by default, whereas the validity of their claim is often confirmed at a later date. According to the Press Complaints Commission:

An asylum seeker can only become an 'illegal immigrant' if he or she
remains in the UK after having failed to respond to a removal notice.
(PCC Guidance note on asylum seekers and refugees, October 2003,
quoted in Finney, 2005)

Many are granted refugee status on appeal. The United Nations and
the trade union movement have thus adopted the term 'irregular
migrant' or 'undocumented migrant'. But British journalists and politicians alike continue to contribute to audience misunderstanding,
using an idiom which has long been considered to mislead and to
bolster racial prejudice (NUJ, 2005: 14). The Information Centre
about Asylum and Refugees (ICAR) has also highlighted those
instances where, although the pejorative 'illegal' is not employed,
asylum seekers are included under the general term 'migrants'. The
term, they argue, fosters the sense that 'this group [is] very powerful,
given its size, and investing in it would bring a shade of danger for the
settled community' (ICAR, 2012).

In 2007, the Commission for Racial Equality (CRE) raised concerns
about the media's use of words like 'surge' and 'flood' and the inherently negative associations they convey (Joint Committee on Human
Rights (JHCR), 2007). The Cardiff School of Journalism, tracing
recent trends in media coverage of asylum seekers, recorded 51
different labels employed by journalists to refer to asylum seekers in
Sangatte, near Calais in 2002. These included 'parasites', 'scroungers',
'would-be immigrants' and 'asylum cheats' (Buchanan et al., 2003: 50).
The study also highlighted the development of military metaphors in
these contexts, which fostered the sense of an invasion or attack,
including the phrases 'legions of young men', 'ranks of migrants',
'massing at Calais' and 'looking like a rag tag army of conscripts'
(Buchanan et al., 2003: 50). They also found that statistics were being
exploited to augment this impression of an impending 'threat'. These
'alarmist statistics' were repeatedly exaggerated and unsourced, as, for
example, with the number of 'immigrants' estimated to be at Sangatte,
variously placed at 1,589, 1,800 and 5,000 (2003: 52). The statistics
were being used without contextual analysis of their meaning, and
where official statistics were lacking, speculation and exaggeration
of immigrants (and 'illegal immigrants') had become routine in
some sections of the media (2003: 52). The media were found to

be relying primarily on official sources such as the government and police. Conversely, little space was allotted to refugee voices even via non-government organisations (NGOs), with the voice of women seeking asylum being the least represented. In another study of the Sangatte coverage, Article 19 found that 'The term "flood" appeared a total of nine times ... seven times in articles about Sangatte. Used less frequently were "deluge", "mass exodus" and "mass influx".' They found that this language was not confined to the tabloids, but that it appeared in the broadsheets as well (Article 19, 2003: 51).

Recent research by the Oxford Migration Observatory found that 'respondents indicate asylum as the most commonly chosen answer when questioned about reasons for migrating, whereas asylum seekers are one of the smallest groups among immigrants (4%)' (Migration Observatory, 2011: 10).

Studies, including those on Sangatte, have criticised the omission of a political context, an omission which has the potential to mislead audiences about the causes that lie behind asylum seeking. The Institute for Public Policy Research (IPPR) for example noted in its 2005 audience reception studies that 'Virtually no participant mentioned events such as the wars in Iraq or Afghanistan as potential drivers of asylum' (Lewis, 2005: 14). Alia and Bull's *Media and Ethnic Minorities* discusses refugees among other groups of ethnic minorities in Britain, and highlights a number of 'myths' they say characterise the coverage of asylum. In addition to the 'ineligibility myth' mentioned above, these include the 'cost myth', which empha- sises refugees as a financial burden, the 'social cost myth', which stresses cultural harm to the 'British way of life', and the 'criminality myth', which casts them as criminals or terrorists (2005: 27–8).

James Curran in his *Media and Democracy* (2011) and Roy Greenslade in 'Seeking scapegoats: the coverage of asylum in the press' (2005) both provide examples in which the tabloid press ran a number of false and exaggerated stories in 2003. These accounts focused around the eating of animals that are either considered taboo or are typically protected as symbols of British heritage. Curran describes how:

> The story was judged to be so important that the Sun (July 4, 2003) cleared its front page to reveal that 'Callous asylum seekers are barbe-

4

cuing the Queen's swans', under the banner headline 'SWAN BAKE'.
'Eastern European poachers', the paper reported, 'lure the protected
Royal birds into baited traps, an official Metropolitan Police report
says.' Its continuation story inside the paper recorded unambiguously:
'Police swooped on a gang of East Europeans and caught them red
handed about to cook a pair of swans.'

(Curran, 2011: 17)

Upon closer investigation, it emerged that there had been no arrests,
nor was there a police report, only an internal memo clarifying the
rules on poaching. Nick Medic, a Serbian exiled journalist who
initiated the complaint and wrote to the police, quoted a letter he
received from Det. Supt. Tristram Hicks saying:

Nobody has been arrested or charged in relation to offences against
swans. The Sun ... referred to asylum seekers being responsible. We
have no information at all that supports this contention and indeed
when we spoke to [the reporter], he agreed that this was a mistake.

(quoted in Medic, 2004)

This was sent on to the Press Complaints Commission (PCC), which
concluded that the paper 'could provide no evidence for the story'
(Curran, 2011: 17). By means of clarification, five months later the
PCC compelled the *Sun* to issue a clarification on p. 41 stating merely
that 'nobody has been arrested in connection with these offences', a
statement which failed to acknowledge that there was no evidence
asylum seekers were responsible (Medic, 2004).

Oxfam has outlined how negative portrayals of asylum seekers in
the media impact directly on communities in terms of harassment
and racial abuse (JCHR, 2007: 99). In a study conducted in 2003
at King's College London (KCL), ICAR discussed the possible links
between media coverage of this kind and patterns of social tension
within communities, including 'racist attacks and street harassment'.
ICAR highlighted a series of alarmist headlines, which included the
following key words:

- arrested, jailed, guilty
- bogus, fraud, illegal
- failed, rejected.

The report found that the language used in racist incidents 'appeared to mirror themes current in the newspapers under study' (Casciani, 2004). Intriguingly, the research conducted by ICAR indicated that local coverage of asylum and immigration is likely to be more positive and less hostile than national coverage. In 2005, ICAR observed that London's local newspapers 'do not tend to comment on policy and are mainly concerned with positive local interactions between individual asylum seekers/refugees and host community members'. It concluded that, in contrast to national coverage, in London's local press:

> There is no appetite for generically linking asylum seekers/refugees to crime, and concerns that asylum seekers are a burden or get preferential treatment are outweighed by belief in their contribution to London's economy and culture. Inflammatory, extreme and fear-inducing language is avoided and articles are well-sourced; a wide range of organisations and individuals is used as sources.
>
> (ICAR, 2005)

In 2007, the JCHR study conducted for the Commission for Racial Equality (CRE) described media coverage as 'potentially shaping the way in which sections of the public viewed asylum seekers, refugees, new migrants and even ethnic minorities more broadly' (JCHR, 2007:99).

UK media coverage has also been criticised for exaggerating the number of refugees applying to the United Kingdom for asylum. The UK Independent Race Monitor's Report in 2005 stated that 'repeated reference to abuse and reducing the numbers of asylum applicants tend to reinforce popular misconceptions that abuse is enormous in scale when in fact it is a small proportion of people who enter the UK' (Coussey, 2005: 100). This misconception appears to be especially prevalent among journalists. According to a study produced by the Cardiff School of Journalism, the journalists interviewed expressed their suspicions that 'asylum seekers' were often in reality economic migrants, though they could provide no evidence to support this belief (Gross, Moore and Threadgold, 2007: 45–6). This study also questioned the failure of journalists to follow up on the deportation of 'failed asylum seekers'. This was explained in terms of both cost and safety, raising the question why refugees seeking asylum are deported to locations from which it would be too dangerous for journalists to report (Gross et al., 2007: 55–6).

Intriguingly, certain journalists in the right-wing press have attempted to resist the way in which they are instructed to cover asylum stories. Greenslade notes that in 2004, following a series of stories in the *Express* regarding what was referred to as an 'invasion' of Roma asylum seekers, the paper's own journalists took 'the unprecedented step of writing to the Press Complaints Commission to complain about being put under pressure by their senior executives to write slanted articles' (Greenslade, 2005: 22). This was not their first attempt to address working practice within the *Express*: in August 2001 the paper's union members complained of its 'sustained campaign against asylum seekers in pursuit of circulation' (Greenslade, 2005: 22). Greenslade notes that 'After some consideration, the PCC said it could not intervene citing its role as a body dealing with complaints from members of the public not from journalists' (2005: 22).

Coverage of asylum in these papers is extensive. A survey in 2002, which examined twelve weeks of coverage in seven major newspapers, found that by far the most articles concerning asylum seekers were found in the *Daily Mail* and the *Express*. In the *Daily Mail* this made up 25 per cent of the paper's total content, and in the *Express* 24 per cent (Article 19, 2003: 14–15). The Glasgow Media Group has also flagged up the danger of such media portrayals as enabling and providing 'a rationale for changes in asylum law' (Philo and Beattie, 1999: 196). The Cardiff School of Journalism underscored these concerns in 2003, saying that 'the relentless repetition of dramatic headlines which speak of an asylum "crisis" has undoubtedly influenced the presentation of successive government policies which have sought, above all, to reduce the number of asylum seekers entering the country' (Buchanan et al., 2003: 12).

Asylum laws have indeed undergone substantial changes intended to regulate the number of applicants successfully claiming asylum in Britain (Hauser, 2000). On a more specific level, the UK Independent Race Monitor's Report has raised concerns as to whether 'hostile, inaccurate and derogatory' media coverage could also influence individual decisions made by immigration caseworkers, 'as it makes caution and suspicion more likely' (Coussey, 2005: 100). The JCHR reiterated this point in 2007, warning of the potential for 'hostile reporting ... to influence the decision making of officials and Government policy' as well as a possible link between such reporting and 'physical attacks on asylum seekers' (2007: 101).

We can thus identify some very clear patterns emerging in media coverage in terms of the subjects covered or avoided and the specific news angles taken. When we began our work in this area we interviewed a series of journalists to assess how the subject of asylum and refugees was being discussed in newsrooms.

Comments from Journalists

We spoke with seven journalists from the BBC, the *Daily Mirror*, the *Star*, Associated Press and other news outlets including broadsheets. Their views were given under conditions of confidentiality. They made very pertinent comments about the conditions under which stories are produced and what they saw as the routine assumptions with which journalists work. These comments fell into three broad areas: story content and news angles; the nature of newsrooms and decisions about the inclusion of stories; and assumptions about readers and audiences.

With regard to the first of these categories, a journalist from a tabloid spoke of the demonisation of asylum seekers, migrants and refugees and how they were consistently treated as a single negative category of people:

> Certainly when it comes to the idea of illegal immigrants and asylum seekers, very often they are just interchangeable terms. There's no attempt ever made to explain what these terms mean. The message always is that they're bad. The idea that an asylum seeker is not an illegal immigrant is completely lost, they are all a problem.

In this way asylum seekers, migrants and refugees join a list of stigmatised peoples and can thus be equated with other ethnic and social minorities. As the journalist notes:

> You know, there's nothing better than a Muslim asylum seeker, in particular, that's a sort of jackpot I suppose. You know, it is very much the cartoon baddy, the caricature, you know, all social ills can be traced back to immigrants and asylum seekers flooding into this country.

Another journalist commented on how the language of asylum and refugees had become linked to external issues such as the seeking of benefits:

> The language itself, the difference between refugee and asylum seeker. You don't hear the word refugee any more, it's asylum seeker all the time. It's been re-classed as somebody looking for benefits.

Some journalists spoke of severe problems with the accuracy of stories. One journalist working for a broadsheet had decided, on a personal impetus, to fact-check stories appearing in the tabloids. This interviewee noted in particular how the immigration figures used therein consistently exaggerated the number of migrants who were living in the United Kingdom. Another journalist, who had worked on a tabloid, made the point that inaccuracy often derives from information that has been deliberately excluded from a story. The idea is to leave out any elements that contradict the main theme that is being pursued:

> I have been told in a newsroom, leave that line out and that line out, then we have got a story – leave out the bits that didn't suit.

The journalist gave this illustration from a story about Muslims snubbing war heroes:

> You know there's an angle you can take, or there's some facts which you can cut out or you can reposition some facts.... it had been a St. George's Cross medal ceremony in which two Respect [people] who were Muslims, hadn't got up and applauded. So that ran ... the fact that Muslims had snubbed our war heroes. What was not mentioned in any of the stories was that there was loads of other Muslims there from all sorts of different political parties who did stand up and applaud, but by completely just removing that one fact it became a situation where it seemed like the only Muslims that were in the room weren't applauding.

Journalists also spoke to us about the nature of newsrooms and the conditions under which they worked. These varied depending upon the maturity and status of journalists. Those who are older or employed as staff reporters are more able to exert some authority over what they cover. As one of the interviewees commented, younger journalists are in a weaker position:

> It's not a meritocracy, it's authoritarian – you do what you're told. It's an authoritarian system in a way, you're just told how to write and if you don't write it in the way they want then it's only going to come back to you to write it again.

An example was given of a woman who had criticised the stories about asylum seekers:

> She very openly spoke out and said 'I don't want to write these kinds of stories, you know, I don't want to do this.' As a result, she got absolutely, sort of, screamed off the news room floor and for the next couple of weeks she was given every anti-Muslim, anti-asylum seeker story to do, every single one until she just resigned.

As another journalist from a major broadsheet observed, so fierce is the competition among younger journalists to climb the career ladder that they require little coercion to write such stories. Rather, their desire to progress professionally is encouragement enough:

> Invariably it's the younger reporters who are sent out to do these sorts of monstering jobs – because they want to get on. The newsroom is an authoritarian place. A more experienced reporter could refuse. One editor had a terrible reputation for bullying but the imbalance between news editor and young inexperienced reporter is enough to get the person to put their conscience aside and go and monster an asylum seeker.

This journalist also noted how they would typically use a reporter from an Asian background so that the paper 'covered itself':

> In general the approach used to be to use young reporters of Asian background to 'do their own'. [A reporter] was used to do a lot of these stitch-up jobs on asylum seekers. The paper wants to cover itself by using a reporter of an ethnic background to do these sort of jobs.

The journalists interviewed also revealed the difficulties of covering stories which offered an alternative perspective. One journalist who worked on a tabloid generally thought to be on the left of the political spectrum commented on a specific story:

I had to fight very hard for stories that were sympathetic to refugees or asylum seekers. I was smuggled into an asylum holding centre and interviewed a woman who had been sex-trafficked and was facing deportation, but it was still hard to get that published.

A third crucial issue discussed here was how assumptions in the news room about the beliefs of readers and audiences affected the choice of stories and the news angles that were taken. As one journalist put it:

There's an assumption in the news desk that the readers will believe that there are not enough jobs, that there are simply too many people coming in, there are too many problems in our own country and it's difficult to put in sympathetic stories on asylum or refugees.

It is also the case that some journalists share the assumptions that are imputed to the readers and viewers. A senior BBC journalist commented to us on his own view that the problems of 'genuine' refugees had been compounded because of the numbers of economic migrants who had sought to claim asylum. Another spoke to us about how many refugees were coming to Britain:

If we did a story about Rwanda or suffering, these readers would think 'It's very sad that it is happening but why are they coming here?' They would think 'Why do most people come to Britain?'

In fact, only a small minority of refugees in the world come to the United Kingdom. Most do not have the funds or resources to travel to developed countries, and refugees more commonly remain in the countries neighbouring those from which they have been displaced.

To what extent then is media coverage of asylum and asylum seekers, which conflates the issue with that of economic migration, helping to fuel hostile attitudes towards refugees? The journalists with whom we spoke were reflective about their own work, and indicated that there was at least some discussion in their newsrooms about the impact of particular stories. But there is a pressing need for a deeper investigation of the impact of media on society as a whole, of the construction and development of public belief, of the inter-action between media agendas and the actions of the state, and the consequences of this for particular communities. This book responds to this, and to calls for more investigation into media content and its impacts from the UN High Commissioner for Refugees, UK politicians, academics, and NGOs such as the Refugee Council and the International Red Cross.

1

A Brief History of Contemporary Migration and Asylum

The Political, Economic and Environmental Contexts of Migration

According to the International Association for the study of Forced Migration (IAFM), the term 'forced migration' suggests 'the movements of refugees and internally displaced people (those displaced by conflicts) as well as people displaced by natural or environmental disasters, chemical or nuclear disasters, famine, or development projects'. Already the 21st century has seen the major displacement and concomitant migration of populations, to which multiple factors have contributed. These can broadly be divided into economic, environmental and conflict-based factors.

Although historically these factors have always affected the movement of populations, it was only in the wake of the Second World War, with the displacement of 40 million refugees across Europe, that an international agreement was struck in an attempt to manage and regulate this phenomenon. The Convention Relating to the Status of Refugees was established in 1951 to enable a basic safeguard for the millions of refugees then scattered across Europe. The Convention offers protection for those forced to seek refuge in another country based on 'well-founded fear of persecution on account of race, religion, nationality, membership in a political social group, or political opinion' (UNHCR, 1951). In legal terms once this 'well-founded fear' has been established those deemed to be experiencing it are considered 'refugees' and have greater protections; prior to this being confirmed they are referred to as 'asylum seekers'. In 2010 there were around 10.4 million refugees in the world (UNHCR, 2011), and the majority of these were located in the world's poorest countries across Asia and Africa.

There are however situations that result in 'forced migration' but are not covered by the Convention. Disaster-induced displacement, for instance, includes natural disasters – floods, volcanoes, landslides, earthquakes – and environmental change or human-made disasters – deforestation, desertification, global warming, industrial accidents – which are often interrelated. The Convention does not offer protection for people who have been dispossessed under such circumstances, though they may be equally vulnerable and may have as great a need for refuge. The UNHCR is therefore concerned that although 'megatrends are exacerbating conflict and combining in numerous ways today to oblige millions more people to flee their homelands', there are clear 'protection gaps' which leave people without support (UN, 2012). It is crucial to acknowledge that economic need is inseparable from humanitarian need and conflict. UN Secretary-General Ban Ki-moon has noted that:

> Today, conflict and human rights abuses – the traditional drivers of displacement – are increasingly intertwined with and compounded by other factors such as population pressure, food insecurity and water scarcity.
>
> (quoted in Dawn.com, 2012)

UN High Commissioner for Refugees Antonio Guterres has stressed that 'Global displacement is an inherently international problem' which needs 'international solutions – and by this I mainly mean political solutions' (quoted in Dawn.com, 2012). In international politics national self-interest has always been dominant in the policy making of states (see Walt, 2012; Waltz, 1979).

The Global Economy

It is important to note when considering issues of forced migration that the manner in which the global economy works contributes to these forms of migration, and that western capitalist economies and corporations are the beneficiaries of this economic system. Early capitalist economic development theorists saw the 'third world' as in need of 'modernisation' to bring it up to the same stage as the West on a linear path of historical and technological development. Such theories disregarded power relations between developed and developing states as a factor in their poverty, and saw progress as something achieved by countries 'independently' by embracing capitalist systems to encourage growth (see Rostow, 1960; Hoselitz, 1952: 28). The Bretton Woods institutions of the World Bank and International Monetary Fund (IMF) were tasked with providing monetary assistance to promote such 'development' projects, and economic adjustment to free market economic policies that would encourage economic growth and reduce communist influence in the developing world.

The World Bank claims to be 'working for a world free of poverty' (www.worldbank.org). But neo-Marxist writers since the 1960s have pointed to such theories as inherently flawed, as western 'core' countries developed at the expense of the underdeveloped 'periphery' of the third world, through deliberate exploitation, imperialism and slavery (see Gunder Frank, 1966: 27–37). They conclude that, since the conditions of the 'underdevelopment' of regions such as Latin America or Africa were created by their participation in the development of world capitalism, capitalist economic theories cannot provide a solution. Development became a cold war battleground, and Bretton Woods institutions were a tool used to fight socialism and promote economic growth, often at the expense of social development, education, health and so on. Mehmet argues that 'overall mainstream economists have failed to recognize that underdevelopment may be causally linked to (1) monopoly profits, externalities, transaction costs and other "market failures" (Bradhan et. al. 1990), and above all, (2) hidden subjective values embedded in these theories themselves' which often follow ethnocentric principles of perfect rationalism (Mehmet, 1999: 3).

The World Bank and IMF have been heavily criticised[1] from this point of view for imposing 'conditionalities' based upon the 'Washington consensus' of economic liberalisation in exchange for

---

1   See: www.brettonwoodsproject.org

loans. Recipient countries are forced to take on a 'structural adjust-ment' programme (now called a Poverty Reduction Growth Facility) of liberalisation for the financial sector, trade and investment, priva-tisation of nationalised industries and deregulation. These policies have been found to be ineffective and often counterproductive, and have often resulted in reduced provision of basic public services such as health and education, through a move to private industry without support for basic infrastructure.

Developing countries need to nurture their own institutions, and without the ability for a country to determine its own industrial and economic policy it is not possible to encourage the development of responsible self-government. One of the effects of structural adjustment is that developing countries must increase their exports. Usually developing countries can only export basic commodities and raw materials which bring the country low revenues, and the prohibitive costs of technology combined with a lack of infrastructure result in their importing higher-cost finished products from the West. Structural adjustment results in economic growth without a role for developing countries in decision making, without social justice or equality, and without environmental sustainability and political stability.

Trade agreements that favour the developed world have also had a major impact. Until 1997, for example, the European Union had special agreements with banana producers in former colonies in the Caribbean. The United States, during the 'banana wars' of the 1990s, successfully fought these on the grounds that they broke free trade rules. The deal had protected Caribbean farmers from competing with Latin American producers whose bananas were grown on large-scale industrial plantations operated by US corporations. Rather than increasing living standards, the opening up of economies in the developing world to foreign multinational investment has caused great damage to these countries, taking away protections for local industry (BBC News, 2009b).

The extraction of raw materials and cheap labour sourced in the developing world by multinational companies has occurred without protections for workers. Structural adjustment programmes mean labour laws and workers' protections (considered sacrosanct in the West) must be removed in these countries to make resources and labour cheaper and increase the profitability of investment for multinationals. The resulting impact of companies like Nike and high-street stores sourcing clothes cheaply in sweatshops in the developing world has been well documented. The environmental impacts of multinational 'investment' have often also been disastrous, and 'development' initiatives have often resulted in people being forced from their land to enable mining, and deforestation for large-scale agricultural development. The production process employed by the Coca-Cola company, for example, led to the draining of local water supplies in India and Mexico, impacting on subsistence farming and local health, and forcing people to buy Coca-Cola as there was no water to drink (Killer Coke, nd; PBS, 2008).

The developing world is also prevented from competing globally by Europe's common agricultural policy, which brings subsidies to European farmers and support for European environmental and rural development. This gives a global advantage to European agriculture to the detriment of African and South American countries, according to the Overseas Development Institute. As Ruth Bergan from the Trade Justice Movement points out, 'The biggest problem is that subsidies keep prices artificially low, mainly for grain traders, so developing country farmers cannot compete' (*Guardian*, 2011b). The environmental impact of large-scale fishing industries with technologically advanced trawlers and industrial long-line fishing, which is resulting in the reduction of world fish stocks by around 70–90 per cent, has caused fishing industries to collapse globally. This is disproportionately affecting those reliant on traditional methods, while corporations able to invest in advanced technologies maximise their take. According to the 2009 documentary *End of the Line*, 'the mouth of the largest trawling net in the world is big enough to accommodate thirteen 747s'. The documentary cited a study for the House of Lords which found that '50 per cent of the cod caught in the North Sea was illegal' (End of the Line, 2009). Blue fin tuna are similarly being illegally fished to extinction, and 60 per cent of those caught are bought by the Mitsubishi company, which is increasing its capacity.

All of this has an impact on migration, as developing countries are increasingly impoverished and unable to sustain even subsistence living. The human effects can be seen in Senegal, where foreign fleets have wiped out fishing for local fishermen (End of the Line, 2009). The increasing scarcity of resources exacerbates the problems faced by such countries, and fuels conflict in many regions of the globe.

Western economic interests have also contributed to global conflicts by financing corrupt leaderships in Africa and South America. The diamond industry in Sierra Leone is just one example. Western consumerism currently fuels the fighting and persecution of local people in eastern Congo. Coltan is a mineral (often mined using child labour) used in the manufacture of electronic circuits (in for example laptops, mobile phones and weapon systems). It is sourced in the Congo, where the economy depends on it, but the income it generates is funding the Hutu militia responsible for the Rwandan genocide, who began controlling the area after being forced from Rwanda in 1994 (Hayes and Burge, 2003; *Blood Coltan*, 2008). Western foreign policies are therefore, in a quest to boost their own economic growth and under pressure from multinationals, financing the conflicts that are causing the world refugee problem. These conflicts are also sustained by lucrative arms exports from the West.

Western arms-producing countries have increasingly brought in arms control measures aimed at ensuring arms are not sold to developing countries responsible for human rights abuses. The United States issued its commitment to these principles in Presidential Directive 34 in 1995, and the former UK foreign secretary Robin Cook claimed in 1997 that 'Labour will not permit the sale of arms to regimes that might use them for internal repression or international aggression' (quoted in Perkins and Neumayer, 2010: 4). But Perkins and Neumayer found that 'the US is by far the largest supplier of arms to developing countries, accounting for close to 40% of transfers between 1992 and 2004', followed by Russia, France, Germany and the United Kingdom (2010: 3). Sales to developing countries accounted for roughly $185 billion of the total $269 billion arms exports (2010: 3). Between 1994 and 2004 it was found that 'human rights abusing countries are actually more likely to receive weapons from the US, while autocratic regimes emerge as more likely recipients of weaponry from France and the UK' (2010: 15). A large proportion of US sales go to Israel, a projected '$30 billion from 2009–2018' which represents an annual average increase of 25 per cent (Reubner, 2011).

In 2005 Gordon Brown visited Tanzania and told the *Daily Mail* 'the days of Britain having to apologise for its colonial history are over', suggesting that we should 'celebrate much of our past rather than apologise for it' (Brogan, 2005). Such statements imply that 'third world' problems are caused independently of western actions, which are seen as wholly positive. They can be used to bolster orientalist notions of states as 'war-like' or incompetent, in contrast to the advanced and peace-loving West. In considering asylum issues it is important for journalists to look beyond the rhetoric of 'humanitarian intervention' and 'human rights' claims, and recognise that the full range of western countries' political actions involves the creation of humanitarian need. The globally perceived hypocrisy means hostility to the West has reached a high point and only a real policy change, not a change of rhetoric, will alter the way developed countries such as the United Kingdom are seen internationally.

Asylum and Immigration in the United Kingdom

Over the 20 years from the early 1990s to date, geopolitical and geo-economic changes as noted above have led to an escalation of the international refugee situation. During the 1980s refugees from Eastern Europe were welcomed into the West. As a proportion of those claiming refugee status, deportations in Britain were low under the Conservative government (Gibney, 2008). At this time, the Labour Party in opposition maintained the stance that the government was too hard on immigrants, particularly refugees (Gibney, 2008). There was a large increase in asylum seekers globally at the end of the cold war, and though global refugee numbers fell after a 1992 peak of 18 million, many countries began to bring in measures to curb the numbers they accepted. The Asylum and Immigration Appeals Act 1993 made the Refugee Convention part of UK law, but this Act also enabled the UK government to detain asylum seekers pending a decision and set strict time limits for appeals. This policy continued with the Asylum and Immigration Act 1996, which introduced restrictions on asylum seekers working, and removed welfare benefit rights from those who had put in their claim for asylum after entering the country. It also introduced a list of 'safe' countries from which all applications would be rejected. Gibney points out that the 'deportation gap' – the difference between the number of people refused asylum and the number deported – became an issue only from 1997 onwards, when New Labour came to power. Before this there was a reluctance to inflict the trauma of deporting someone (Gibney, 2008: 154).

Between 1996 and 2002 UK asylum applications increased from 29,640 to a peak of 84,130 applications in 2002 (Blinder, 2011). New Labour policy was heavily attacked during this time by the opposition leader William Hague, who argued that the increasing numbers represented 'organised abuse' of the asylum system by economic migrants (quoted by BBC News, 2000a). Labour was accused of being weak on border control, and the issue of deportations was pushed by both Hague and shadow home secretary Anne Widdecombe. Political and media debate built on concern that there might be links between the numbers of 'failed' asylum seekers in the country (the 'deportation gap') and 'illegal immigration', and this came to dominate public debate. This was a concern and an interpretation which both main parties accepted, marking a consensus between them about what were seen as the problems, if not the solutions. Blair accepted that there was 'abuse' of the asylum system as a result of 'illegal immigration' with an economic motivation. He sought to appear strong on this perceived

---

Key Legislation

Asylum and Immigration Appeals Act (1993)
Asylum and Immigration Act (1996)
Human Rights Act (1998)
Immigration and Asylum Act (1999)
Nationality, Immigration and Asylum Act (2002)
Asylum and Immigration (Treatment of Claimants, etc.) Act (2004)
Immigration, Asylum, and Nationality (IAN) Act (2006)
UK Borders Act (2007)
Criminal Justice and Immigration Act (2008)
Borders, Citizenship and Immigration Act (2009)

'abuse' by tightening the asylum system (Gibney, 2008: 156). New Labour thus produced a 1998 White Paper that aimed to 'maximise efficiency and minimise the scope for abuse' (Home Office, 1998).

The Conservative Party in opposition made asylum 'abuse' and deportations a key issue in the 2000 local elections. Hague argued that 'People are arriving in Britain armed with expert knowledge of how to exploit our asylum laws; what to say on arrival; how to string out appeals and how to remain here if their cases are eventually turned down' (quoted by BBC News, 2000a).

Further legislation was brought in to regulate the number coming to the United Kingdom to claim asylum and the applications of people seeking asylum when already in the United Kingdom, as well as their welfare entitlements. Labour's Immigration and Asylum Act 1999 allowed asylum seekers to be dispersed nationwide, and made a new National Asylum Support Agency responsible for supporting asylum seekers during an asylum claim or while awaiting the result of an appeal. It extended the offences of entering the country by deception, and introduced severe penalties for agents who clandestinely brought people into the country. At the same time deportations were increasing – between 1993 and 2003 the number of failed applicants deported (excluding dependants) rose from 1,820 to 13,500 (Gibney, 2008: 149).

The spike in asylum applications to the United Kingdom in 2002 (see Figure 1.1) which drove the debate about asylum 'abuse' and 'illegal immigration' was linked in public discussion to events during the summer of 2001 at Sangatte, France. A Red Cross humanitarian shelter was set up during the Kosovo crisis for refugees seeking asylum, who had previously been sleeping rough in Calais. It became overcrowded, and some of the refugees were filmed trying to jump aboard Eurotunnel trains at Sangatte on Christmas Day. Eurotunnel claimed it stopped 18,500 refugees trying to smuggle themselves into the United Kingdom in the first six months of 2001 (*Guardian*, 2002b). The spike in applications coincided with increased media coverage; in July a MORI poll showed this issue generated high public concern. This prompted the UK government to make a deal with France to close the Sangatte centre in 2002, forcing the asylum seekers back onto the Calais streets.

Tony Blair made it his priority to 'deliver a radical reduction in

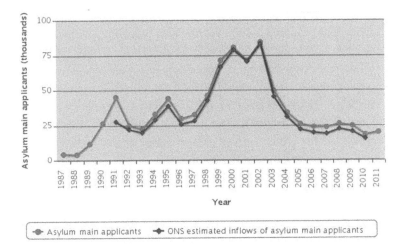

Figure 1.1 UK Asylum applications and estimated inflows, 1987–2011

Source: Blinder (2011) (using a chart from Oxford Migration Observatory, with original data from the Office for National Statistics on long-term international migration).

the number of unfounded asylum applications' as well as a focus on deportations (quoted in Milne and Travis, 2002). But the debate on Sangatte failed to recognise another significant source for the increased refugee migration in 2002: the war against Afghanistan. In the wake of Sangatte, the terrorist attacks of 11 September 2001 led to the displacement of people fleeing war and drove up asylum numbers. This also drove concern about border controls and calls for enhanced security measures and checks on those entering the country. The Home Secretary David Blunkett said that 'it is our task to ensure that terrorists cannot pose as asylum seekers or avail themselves of the protection of the Geneva Convention' (2003). Driven by war, 9,000 asylum seekers arrived from Afghanistan during 2001 – around 50 per cent of them unaccompanied children (Jones, 2010). The US invasion of Iraq further drove up asylum numbers, with 1.5 million Iraqis given refuge. Refugees mainly sheltered in neighbouring countries, but many also came to Europe, where Sweden took the most (*Der Spiegel*, 2007).

The UK Nationality, Immigration and Asylum Act 2002 abolished 'exceptional leave to remain', a provision whereby some asylum seekers in exceptional circumstances could obtain permission to stay for up to four years. The Act removed asylum seekers' right to work, and Section 55 removed National Asylum Support Service (NASS) support for asylum seekers who had failed to make a claim 'as soon as reasonably practicable' after arriving in the country, leaving thousands without income (Clements, 2007). Beyond terrorism, fears of increased criminality were also contributing to a wider sense of concern in relation to asylum numbers. Chris Fox, president of the Association of Chief Police Officers, claimed in 2003 that foreign criminals 'from the Nigerian fraudster and the eastern European who deals in drugs and prostitution to the Jamaican concentration on drug dealing' were increasingly using asylum to travel around the world (Thompson, 2003). Humanitarian groups and politicians disputed the validity of this claim, saying asylum seekers were no more likely to be criminals than anyone else, but concern remained (Refugee Action, 2012). Despite large global refugee numbers and the United Kingdom's responsibility for the ongoing war in Afghanistan, Tony Blair announced in February 2003 that UK asylum applications would be halved by September 2003 (*Guardian*, 2003).

Blair's goal to reduce applications embodied the widely held perception that the numbers of asylum seekers entering the United Kingdom constituted both an economic burden and a post-9/11 security threat, although this perspective was challenged by politicians, legal opinion and refugee organisations (see Chapter 2). Recent statistics on asylum show that Blair's reduction target was more than met, with only 33,960 asylum applications received in 2004 (Blinder, 2011). Yet concern remained, and Blair promised in 2004 to 'remove more each month than apply' and 'restore faith in a system that we know has been abused' (Blair, 2004). At this time Michael Howard, the Conservative opposition leader, pushed to withdraw from the 1951 UN Convention and send away all genuine refugees beyond a set quota, but suggestions of turning away genuine refugees were contentious. The Commission for Racial Equality published a report in 2005 that claimed there was widespread public hostility toward asylum seekers, who were seen as a burden on the country (Finney and Peach, 2005: 28). Considering the reduction in asylum applications one of its successes, New Labour fought the 2005 General

Election campaign on the issue of asylum. To address public concern it pledged 'Your country's borders protected: I.D. cards and strict controls that work to combat asylum abuse and illegal immigration.'

The bombings of 7 and 21 July 2005 further heightened tensions over asylum and immigration. In response to this, and under pressure from the United States (Hope and Blake, 2011), Blair's '12-point' plan promised strict control of borders. It pledged to reject asylum claims from anyone who had induced or 'participated in terrorism anywhere', and would enable people to be stripped of citizenship if it was 'in the public good' (Prince, 2010). David Blunkett in 2005 launched 'citizenship' tests for immigrants to ensure their 'Britishness' in response to concerns about social cohesion. All this paved the way for the 2006 Immigration, Asylum and Nationality Act, and later the 2007 Borders Act. A five-year plan was laid out with strong measures to control borders. The Immigration, Asylum and Nationality Act 2006 also increased the penalties on anyone employing people illegally. The Act increased the difficulty of obtaining citizenship and extended the qualifying period to eight years. It sought 'to ensure that newcomers to the United Kingdom earn the right to stay' (*Guardian*, 2009b). Asylum seekers would no longer be permitted to stay permanently. If granted refugee status they would receive temporary leave to remain for up to five years. This term could be renewed, but it would restrict refugees' ability to plan long-term and affect their employment prospects (Refugee Council, 2010a). Similarly restrictive policies were brought in for economic migrants. A 'points system' was introduced under which the most skilled people could obtain work permits, to 'only allow into Britain the people and skills our economy needs' (Blair quoted in Home Office, 2005b).

Blair's 2003 pledge had foreshadowed a steady decline in applications, which fell to as low as 23,608 main applicants in 2006 (Blinder, 2011). Deportations of 'failed' asylum seekers increased to 18,235 (JCHR, 2007), something Blair held up as 'enormous progress' (*Guardian*, 2006a). This occurred at a time of increasing global need for asylum. At the time UNHCR data shows that between 2005 and 2006 there was a 56 per cent increase in the number of 'refugees, asylum seekers, internally displaced peoples, returned refugees and stateless persons' globally (with a 2006 figure of over 34 million)

(Oxfam, 2007). While the global number of actual 'refugees' was low, the changing shape of 'need' according to the UN High Commissioner for Refugees meant that 'forced displacement for political, economic and environmental reasons' was going to be one of the 21st century's biggest problems (Campbell, 2006).

By 2007 UNHCR data revealed that 'the conflicts in Iraq and Afghanistan accounted for more than half of the world's refugees', forced from their countries by US and British-led conflicts (Cumming-Bruce, 2008). But in Britain there was growing public debate over the feared criminality and terrorist dangers posed by asylum seekers. There was increasing concern from the UNHCR that 'states will use the issue of terrorism to legitimise the introduction of restrictive asylum practices and refugee policies, a process which began well before the events of September 11 2001' (Campbell, 2006). In May, Blair criticised a controversial legal decision to allow nine Afghan hijackers' asylum claims and David Cameron told the media that if elected to government he would 'reform, replace or scrap' the Human Rights Act to enable authorities to have more flexibility and control (BBC News, 2006a). New Labour's 1998 Human Rights Act incorporated the European Convention on Human Rights into UK law, giving human rights the status of 'higher law', which in cases of conflict would overrule national legislation. Essentially, it meant that people in the United Kingdom could rely on the protections in the European Convention on Human Rights without going all the way to the European courts.

Following the hijacker case and further inflaming the debate came Charles Clarke's ousting from the position of Home Secretary when it was made known that 1,023 'foreign prisoners' had been released by the authorities without being considered for deportation. Among these were a group of nine foreign prisoners who had been convicted of serious offences including murder, manslaughter, rape and child sex offences. Blair spoke at Prime Minister's Questions about deporting the criminals, saying:

> In the vast bulk of cases, as was explained, there will be an automatic presumption now to deport – and the vast bulk of those people will indeed be deported. Those people, in my view, should be deported irrespective of any claim that they have that the country to which they

are going back may not be safe and that is why it is important, as I say, if necessary, that we look at legislating to ensure that such an automatic presumption applies.

(BBC 6 *O'Clock News*, 17 May 2006)

This intention to deport people to countries considered unsafe echoed Cameron's earlier comments, as it raised the issue of withdrawal from the Human Rights Act and European Convention, which would be necessary if what Blair suggested was to be done. Clarke's replacement John Reid declared shortly afterwards that the UK Border Agency was 'not fit for purpose', and restated that those convicted of a serious offence 'should be deported – full stop' (BBC News, 2006c).

The shadow minister for immigration, Damian Green, raised the question of whether the government's controversial system had preoccupied the Immigration and Nationality Directorate (IND), distracting them from concern with the deportation of 'foreign criminals' (Press Association, 2006). Yet the debate about how many 'failed asylum seekers' were being deported continued, and when asked by the Home Affairs Select Committee how many people he estimated to be in the UK illegally, Dave Roberts, head of enforcement at the IND, replied 'I haven't the faintest idea' (Roberts, 2006). Questions were raised about the Border Agency's competence in removals. 'Embarkation controls' then emerged as a matter of debate, as it was unclear how many people had left. Labour's 1998 removal of these checks on people leaving the country was frequently referred to in criticism by the shadow minister for immigration Damian Green in 2006, although the Conservative Party itself had begun to remove these controls in 1994.

Reid subsequently revealed that a backlog existed of 450,000 asylum cases, which he claimed would be cleared within five years (*Guardian* (1), 2 June 2011). Facing opposition claims that the Border Agency UK was in chaos, the Borders Act 2007 was brought in, and narrowed the grounds on which deportation could be prevented. A direct response was made to the 'foreign criminals' story: automatic deportation followed for foreign nationals who had been imprisoned for specific offences or for longer than one year. The Borders Act also made provision for compulsory biometric identity documents for non-EU immigrants and gave immigration officers police-like powers, including increased detention, entry, search and seizure powers. Immigrants granted limited leave to remain faced additional reporting and residency conditions. Immigration minister Liam Byrne claimed this Act would 'give immigration officers vital new powers to do their job better, to secure our borders, tackle the traffickers and shut down illegal working' (*Guardian*, 2009a). Human rights group Liberty have argued however, that the Act was an 'unwelcome departure from the traditional approach in both criminal and immigration matters of judging each case on its particular merits' and the immigration officers' new powers could prove 'socially and racially divisive' (*Guardian*, 2009a). The UNHCR also underscored the importance of the Border Agency, recognising the 'individual difficulties' faced by asylum seekers and their families arriving in great humanitarian need who frequently do not have access to their documents (2008: 11).

The number of asylum applications has continued to fall (see Figure 1.1), but in 2011 the issue of the 2006 backlog, decisions and thus deportations reentered the debate. It was revealed in a Commons Home Affairs Select Committee report that 40 per cent of the 2006 backlog of 450,000 cases had been allowed to stay in the United Kingdom by the new Coalition Government and just 9 per cent of applicants had been rejected, leading to accusations that there had been a 'backdoor amnesty' on asylum (*Guardian*, 2011a). It had proved impossible to trace 74,500 applicants. Labour's Gerry Sutcliffe concluded from the report that there were 'not sufficient resources to track and return illegal immigrants' (*Guardian*, 2011a). People were allowed to stay in many cases because of the length of time they had been in the country; it had taken so long to process their claims that many had acquired families in the United Kingdom. Jonathan Ellis of the Refugee Council declared this was the 'most humane thing to do' especially as many asylum seekers had been left 'in limbo' for so long (*Guardian*, 2011a). War is the greatest cause of this kind of displacement. People seeking asylum in Europe (including the United Kingdom) during 2011 came from the former Yugoslavia, Afghanistan, Iraq, Turkey, Somalia, Democratic Republic of Congo, Zimbabwe and Sri Lanka, but originating countries change according to world events.

Immigration secretary Damian Green denied there had been an 'amnesty'. He said 'The main thing is we've now eliminated this backlog from the system' (*Guardian*, 2011a). But the report criticised a slight decrease in 'the percentage of applicants and dependants sent home' during that year, and from this Keith Vaz, the committee chair, concluded that the Border Agency was 'still not fit for purpose' (*Guardian*, 2011a).

Debate was still focused on how many asylum seekers could be 'sent home'. Migration Watch along with Nicholas Soames MP (Conservative) and Frank Field MP (Labour) criticised the rise in 'net migration' during 2011, saying this meant 'the Government clearly needs to act urgently' (Eaton, 2011). Yet this rise was, according to the *New Statesman* and government figures, due to falling emigration, with immigration having remained stable since 2004 (Eaton, 2011). In 2011 the United Kingdom only received 19,804 asylum applications, but according to an UNHCR (2011) report, the number of refugees globally was the highest since 2000. The latest British Social Attitudes Survey shows that 'just over half, 51%, of the population think immigration should reduce "a lot"' compared with 35 per cent in 1995, a statistic which implies that these debates and how they are covered in the media will remain significant for some time to come (Rogers, 2012).

2

Methods, Explanations and Perspectives on Asylum

In the 1990s migration and the alleged 'threats' that it posed were a focus of some public debate, and during the subsequent decade there was a growing emphasis on linking this debate to the issue of asylum. In this section we analyse media coverage, focusing on major news stories which appeared in the press and on television. Before doing so we identify the range of arguments in public debate about asylum and migration. Within each area of debate there are competing perspectives. A key part of our method is first to establish what perspectives there are, and then to examine how they appear as themes in news accounts. We show how some are dominant and others are absent or appear only as fragments or brief references. This is the core of our approach, known as thematic analysis. We begin then with our outline of key themes in this area.

Methods

For the study of media content which follows, we employed both qualitative and quantitative methods. Our approach is based on the assumption that in any controversial area there will be a range of contested perspectives. These often relate to different political positions, and can be seen as ideological if they relate to the legitimation of ways of understanding which are linked to social interests. Our method begins by setting out the range of available arguments in public discourse on a specific subject. We then analyse the news texts to establish which of these appear and how they do so in the flow of news programming and press coverage. Some may be referenced only occasionally or in passing, while others occupy a much more dominant position, for example being highlighted in news headlines or in interview questions or editorials. Some arguments and the assumptions that they contain, for example that a 'large number' of migrants constitute a 'threat', may underpin the structure of specific news stories. This is in the sense that the story is organised around this way of understanding migration, and the different elements of the story, for example interviewees, the information quoted, the selection of images and editorial comment, all work to elaborate and legitimise threat as a key theme. In past research we have shown, using this method, that news accounts can and do operate to establish specific ways of understanding.

News may appear as a fast and sometimes chaotic flow of information and comment, but it is also underpinned by key assumptions about social relationships and how they are to be understood. At the heart of these are beliefs about motivations, cause and effect, responsibility and consequence. So a newspaper report on people seeking asylum might make assumptions on each of these aspects. The 'real' motive for people coming might be posited as their seeking a better life or economic advantage. Britain is seen as a 'soft touch' for its benefit system, with inadequate laws or administrative structures, and the effect is an uncontrolled 'flood'. The responsibility is with politicians who have failed to stop this so-called 'flood', and the consequences are that great burdens are placed on British society. As we will show, there are many flaws and false assumptions in such a chain of understanding. A central part of our work and our development of new methods has been to show how such key thematic elements and the explanations they embody can be abstracted from news texts and shown to impact upon audience understanding (see for example Philo, 1990; Philo and Berry, 2011).

For the purposes of this study, in our content analysis we break down the text to identify the major subject areas that are pursued in the news, then examine the explanatory frameworks which underpin them. This qualitative approach involves detailed analysis of key explanatory themes in headlines and the text of news programmes and newspaper articles. We examine the preference given to some arguments in that they are highlighted by journalists or are repeatedly used or referred to across news reports. We then make a quantitative assessment of the presence of such themes across news reporting by counting the use of specific phrases and meaningful terms. This is done for each of the news angles in which asylum and refugees are discussed: for example the numbers arriving or deported, immigration controls, 'burdens' on the country, alleged threats posed, and in some coverage the problems faced by refugees.

We also analyse the use of reported statements. We count who is quoted and the nature of their contribution, for example whether they are speaking critically about support for asylum seekers and other migrants (who are often conflated). This is assessed by identifying and counting occurrences of specific language, as with the phrase 'no right to be here', applied to groups whose claims have been rejected. On this basis, we are able to give an account of the exact language used to develop specific themes and the manner in which the dominance of some is established. This is then cross-related to our audience research by a process of asking focus group members to write headlines on the subject of refugees and asylum. We have used this approach in other research, and typically participants are able to reproduce spontaneously from memory the key themes that we have established as present in media accounts.

We conducted four focus groups in areas where there were established migrant groups to examine both perceptions of media coverage and impacts on local communities. In this study we also interviewed seven journalists who provide further evidence of the manner in which the media coverage is structured. Finally we interviewed 36 refugees and professionals who work and have specific expertise in the area. They were asked about both the nature of media coverage and its effects on refugees and those seeking asylum.

Main Explanations and Perspectives on Asylum in the United Kingdom

'Abuse' of the Asylum System by 'Illegal Immigrants'

A dominant theme in both the main parties' explanations of immigration holds that the asylum system is being 'abused' by economic migrants who enter illegally and fraudulently claim asylum without a 'well founded fear of persecution' (UNHCR, 1951). When he was prime minister, Tony Blair accepted that there was 'abuse' of the asylum system because of 'illegal immigration' for economic reasons, and sought a tightening of the system (Gibney, 2008: 156). One example of this is the New Labour White Paper in 1998, which strove to 'maximise efficiency and minimise the scope for abuse' (Home Office, 1998). Political and media debate built on concern that there might be links between numbers of 'failed' asylum seekers in the country, the 'deportation gap' and 'illegal immigration', and this came to dominate public opinion. As was noted in Chapter 1, recognition of this as a concern was a matter of consensus between both main parties.

New Labour was criticised in this area by William Hague as leader of the Conservative opposition in 2000, who argued that there was 'organised abuse' of the asylum system by economic migrants, which put Britain's 'proud tradition' of offering asylum under threat (BBC News, 2000a). Labour was accused of being weak on border control and the issue of deportations. The Conservatives attributed this in part to the loss of 'embarkation controls'. This meant it was unclear how many people had left the country. Labour's 1998 removal (for 'efficiency' reasons) of these checks on people leaving the country was frequently cited as evidence by the shadow minister for immigration Damian Green in 2006, though the Conservative Party itself had began to dismantle them in 1994. However, as mentioned above, the opposition Conservative Party focused on the asylum system 'failures' of the incumbent Labour Party as a key issue.

As we have mentioned, a survey of public opinion in 2005 found a perception that most asylum seekers were not genuine (Finney and Peach, 2005: 28). In response to such pressures, New Labour's 2005 General Election campaign emphasised its concern with asylum issues and moving toward stronger immigration controls. Strict legislation was introduced in response to the assertion that UK asylum laws were weak and open to abuse, including six new parliamentary Acts attributable to Blair.

Alternative Perspectives

Within this explanatory theme, an equivalence is assumed between the number of rejected asylum seekers remaining in the United Kingdom and the number of 'illegal immigrants' in the country. It is assumed that a 'failed asylum seeker' must be an 'illegal immigrant' who tried to 'abuse' the system, although nearly 30 per cent win their case on appeal, and immigration officials have been accused of rejecting people too eagerly (Refugee Council, 2010b).

It is important to note the influence particularly since 2002 of the think-tank Migration Watch in this debate, and its founders Sir Andrew Green and Professor David Coleman. It is frequently cited in the conservative press, and according to research by Powerbase in 2007, it had been named as a source in 2,365 articles since its inception in 2001. While Migration Watch states its support for asylum, there is an assumption made that many cases are not genuine, and Coleman has argued that 'All [asylum] claimants must be detained while their cases are considered, then immediately removed if those cases are rejected' (Pallister, 2007).

Yet Don Flynn of the Joint Council for the Welfare of Immigrants estimated in 2000 that the number of people who seek asylum and later evade detection is a 'tiny fraction' (BBC News, 2000b). The vast majority of undocumented migrants are not those who enter covertly then claim asylum, they are 'overstayers', often from the Commonwealth, who enter legitimately but fail to leave, including (in 2000) 40,000 from Australia (BBC News, 2000b). Since embarkation controls were scrapped, it has become harder to know when people enter legally and then fail to leave. This is why when asked by the Home Affairs Select Committee how many people he estimated were in the United Kingdom 'illegally', Dave Roberts, head of enforcement at the IND, replied 'I haven't the faintest idea' (BBC News, 2006b). But some question whether the restoration of embarkation controls would reduce 'illegal immigration'. The Home Affairs Select Committee argued in 2006 that 'The danger of re-introducing embarkation controls is that it might encourage people to stay illicitly rather than risk being caught at the border for overstaying' (House of Commons, 2006).

The issue of their 'illegal entry' is held as evidence in treating asylum seekers as 'illegal immigrants'. As there is often no way asylum seekers can escape to and enter a safe country by complying with ordinary border controls, the Refugee Convention (of which the United Kingdom is a member) states that:

> The Contracting States shall not impose penalties, on account of their illegal entry or presence, on refugees ... coming directly from a territory where their life or freedom was threatened.
>
> (UNHCR, 1951)

As observed above, the UNHCR stresses that every case is different, and Border Agency officials must recognise that asylum seekers and their families arriving in great humanitarian need may not be able to provide documents (UNHCR, 2008: 11). This makes it very difficult to enter the United Kingdom by a regular route. Research by the Refugee Council in 2008 discussed a legal exchange in 2000 regarding the practice of turning away Czech Roma asylum seekers trying to enter Britain with valid travel documentation: 'despite recognising the persecution of Roma citizens within the Czech Republic [they were turned away] on the alleged grounds that they were not genuinely seeking entry for the purpose stated' (Reynolds and Muggeridge, 2008: 37–8). In court:

> the Immigration Service justified their actions by arguing that the UK is not obliged under the 1951 Refugee Convention to consider applications outside the UK, nor to facilitate travel to the UK for the purpose of applying for asylum ... the House of Lords upheld the Government's position that it is not obliged to consider asylum claims outside its territory in its judgement on the case.
>
> (Reynolds and Muggeridge, 2008: 37–8)

Asylum seekers must therefore enter somehow prior to making their asylum claim, but they may well be travelling without documents and can often be turned away or refused entry. As one of our interviewees, a refugee, stated:

maybe in British people's opinion everyone for them is a criminal because they want to enter to their country illegally but we must understand these people and help them. [Asylum seekers] don't have another way to enter to this country.... these people can arrive without any documents but it's not their mistake it's just simply these people cannot get their passport from their Government, because they leave... their country very fast because their life is in dangerous.

(asylum seeker, Russia)

'Soft Touch' Britain Takes Too Many

A report for the Commission for Racial Equality (CRE) argued in 2005 that there were widespread and long-standing public beliefs that 'Britain is a "soft touch"' and that 'there are too many asylum seekers' (Finney and Peach, 2005: 28). This is an argument frequently used by politicians, who emphasise the numbers of immigrants to justify stronger immigration controls. There is a long precedent for these concerns in British politics, and former Prime Minister Margaret Thatcher was criticised in 1978 when she remarked after a riot in Wolverhampton that the public felt 'that this country might be swamped by people of a different culture' (*Guardian*, 2002a). The perception that the United Kingdom was a 'soft touch' with a weak asylum system that was allowing too many people into the country deepened when the 2002 spike in asylum applications became linked in public debate to asylum seekers entering the United Kingdom from Sangatte, France. That July, a MORI poll showed asylum numbers were second only to health care in public concern. These arguments are often linked to the idea of asylum seekers placing a financial and social burden on the country. In 2009 Sir Andrew Green from Migration Watch was still stating that the numbers of people 'queuing up in Calais' was because Britain was seen as a 'soft touch' and arguing that 80 per cent of applicants had been allowed to stay since 2000 (*Today*, 2009).

The public debate usually assumes that there is a need for control of immigration and borders, often based on the belief that immigration and asylum place a burden on the country. Immigration minister Damian Green for instance has argued that 'many countries around the world ... want immigration and want immigrants but it's got to be planned, and it's got to be controlled' (*Newsnight*, BBC2,

18 May 2006). Many legislative changes by Labour during the 1990s and 2000s were made in the name of immigration control. The belief in immigration control extends across the two main parties and is rarely questioned, though the extent of the controls needed and the means of implementing them are debated. That some control is necessary is also accepted by most international institutions and NGOs. This often extends in political debate to a need for greater immigration controls or a fear that control has been lost.

Alternative Perspectives

The need for increasing immigration controls is built upon the concern that the United Kingdom is taking 'too many' immigrants. But the UNHCR and other critics point out that UK 'immigration controls' are turning away 'genuine' refugees and creating a system biased towards reducing numbers regardless of need (Verkaik, 2006). Asylum applications fell from 84,132 in 2002 to 23,608 in 2006, a 72 per cent reduction, and fell still further by 2011 to 19,804 (Blinder, 2011). That immigration controls are needed at all has actually begun to be more deeply questioned in the light of the changing international pressures of migration. The British 'no borders' campaign is driven by 'no one is illegal' (NOII – see www.noii.org.uk) and a number of academics including Bob Hughes from Oxford Brookes University. The Coalition pledged to reduce immigration dramatically by 2015, but recently the Office for Budget Responsibility has recommended increasing immigration as a solution to the financial crisis facing the country, otherwise the country will face an 'extra £17bn of spending cuts and tax rises to bring down the national debt to 40 per cent of gross domestic product by 2062' (Chu and Grice, 13 July 2012). It also advised that if immigration stayed at current levels the economy would grow more quickly.

Refugee rights groups, NGOs and non-partisan inquiries have constantly challenged the suggestion by the two main political parties that the United Kingdom is a 'soft touch' on asylum and immigration in general. Regarding the Migration Watch statistic, Donna Covey, chief executive of the Refugee Council, points out that fewer than a third of asylum applicants receive any help (*Today*, 2009). As we observe above, the focus of public debate on Sangatte in explaining the spike in refugee migration in 2002 failed to recognise that the people at the camp might genuinely be fleeing the war in Afghanistan. The refugees caused by US-led and European-led conflicts are a continuing problem, and in 2007 there were still a reported 2.1 million refugees from Afghanistan. Those trying to reach the United Kingdom from Sangatte were seen as 'illegal immigrants' fleeing an international conflict the United Kingdom was pursuing.

The UNHCR argued that there is a common misconception that most refugees are taken by western developed countries. In fact 80 per cent of refugees are sheltered in countries neighbouring their home country, with Pakistan taking 2 million refugees in 2007. The United States by contrast took very few given its capacity, only 281,000 (Cumming-Bruce, 2008). When refugees are taken in by developing countries this can lead to instability and future displacements, as these countries of first entry are often struggling themselves. This has lead to calls for developed countries to play a greater role in easing the asylum problem. UNHCR UK spokesman Mans Nyberg said, 'Europe has the impression that the industrialised countries are being flooded. But the flood is into poorer countries. They can't cope. That's why richer countries have to step in to help' (*Guardian*, 2011a). Furthermore, while the two main parties have fought to reduce the numbers of asylum seekers taken by the United Kingdom, the UNHCR has criticised the high number of refusals to grant refuge, and questioned the ability of the asylum procedures to ensure a fair hearing in every case. The UNHCR's most serious criticism was directed at the handling of asylum claims, and included accusations of racial stereotyping and an ignorance of human rights law. One report criticised the practice of using male immigration officers to interview victims of rape, sexual assault, forced marriage or domestic violence. The report observed 'a failure to apply the correct methodology in assessing the facts', resulting in the 'frequent use of speculative arguments' in 'Reasons for refusal letters' (Verkaik, 2006). Contributory factors in this included:

> flawed credibility assessments, an application of the wrong standard of proof, a failure to apply objective country of origin information, the adoption of a narrow UK perspective or a refusal mindset where caseworkers appear to be looking to refuse a claim from the outset.
>
> (Verkaik, 2006)

37

This supports Gibney's claim that although it is possible the disappearance of a 'failed' claimant may be because of a weak case and underlying economic motive, as often suggested, doing so:

> may also be a rational move for those with a genuine need for asylum. An asylum seeker may opt for a kind of 'informal asylum', outside the purview of the state, if they do not trust state officials to make fair or accurate decisions on refugee status
>
> (Gibney, 2008: 151)

A Burden on Welfare and the Job Market

The Refugee Convention guarantees refugees 'the same treatment as is accorded to nationals' within the country of asylum, including residence rights, and access to employment, social welfare, education and housing (UNHCR, 1951). While a large proportion of refugees bring educational qualifications, skills and experience, there is high unemployment and poverty in refugee populations (Refugee Action, 2006). Underlying the beliefs that the United Kingdom takes too many refugees and that many asylum seekers are 'illegal immigrants' (detailed above) is the belief that to accord rights to for example welfare benefits, legal aid, housing and healthcare to asylum seekers creates a burden on the country's resources. Often they are accused of taking British jobs. This was reflected in the claims in the CRE report from 2005, that there was a sustained and widespread public belief that:

- asylum seekers pose a threat to British culture (including religion, values, ethnicity and health)
- asylum seekers pose a threat to the British economy (through illegality, increased competition and an economic burden)
- asylum seekers are treated well to the detriment of the existing population (Finney and Peach, 2005: 28).

This is at times reflected in politicians' discourse, and in 2007 Labour MP Margaret Hodge argued that British-born people should take precedence over new migrants for social housing. The British National Party came out in support, saying that 'Britain is full and there is no more room' (Revill and Doward, 2007). Likewise, Home

Secretary David Blunkett in 2002 described doctors and British schools as 'swamped' and unable to cope with the numbers of asylum seekers they received (*Guardian*, 2002a). Plans were being introduced to remove the asylum seekers from mainstream schools.

This concern extends more widely, and drove the introduction of a 'points system' for economic migrants allowing only the most skilled people to obtain work permits and limiting total immigration. Migration Watch has been featured widely in this debate, arguing that population forecasts are downplayed and immigration is an unsustainable burden to the United Kingdom (Pallister, 2007).

Alternative Perspectives

Chancellor George Osborne's Office for Budget Responsibility watchdog has advised that spending cuts to public services and a fall in economic growth would result if immigration were cut to the levels the Conservatives plan by 2015. It points out that 'if net inward migration were cut to zero over the next five decades, the scale of the public austerity facing Britain would need to be three times larger, at £46 bn' (Chu and Grice, 2012). This is partly because of the ageing UK population; most immigrants are of working age. An ICAR study from 2003 found that 'asylum seekers were more likely to encounter hostility linked to negative reporting if they lived in poor areas where locals believed they may be competing for decent housing' (Casciani, 2004).

According to the Chartered Institute of Housing, asylum seekers' use of social housing is statistically 'very limited' (2008: 2), and Robinson argues that the claims of an unfair advantage in obtaining social housing in the United Kingdom are a 'moral panic' (2009). Justice minister Harriet Harman responded to Margaret Hodge's comments by saying that 'if we have allowed people to be here because they are afraid of persecution or if we need them to work here, then they and their children must be treated equally' (Revill and Doward, 2007).

Refugee rights groups have pointed out that any burden to the state could be eased if asylum seekers were permitted to work. Concern with the burden of asylum seekers claiming benefits led to Section 55 of the 2002 Nationality, Immigration and Asylum Act, which removed NASS welfare support for asylum seekers who had failed to make a claim 'as soon as reasonably practicable' after arriving in the

United Kingdom. Far from being generous, UK welfare benefits, at £62 a week for a single unemployed person, are some of the lowest in Europe, and asylum seekers are entitled to only 70 per cent of this (Faculty of Public Health, 2008). The Refugee Council points out that most refugees know very little about the benefits they will receive before they arrive in the United Kingdom. Many are skilled, and they usually expect that they will be allowed to work and support themselves (Crawley, 2010). However, concerns about their 'taking British jobs' motivated successive legislation denying working rights to asylum seekers and forcing them to rely on the state. In 1996, they were denied the right to work for their first six months in the country. In 2002 they lost all right to work, but since 2005 asylum seekers have been able to work if they have been waiting more than a year for a decision. Crawley argues that such policies have led to an increase in 'poverty, deskilling, loss of self-esteem and significant under- and unemployment, including among those recognised as needing international protection and allowed to remain', as well as 'increased incidents of racism and discrimination directed not only at asylum seekers but towards minority communities in general' (2010: 49–50).

Refugee rights groups have equated destitution to a deliberate deterrent policy by the government, and argue that it is crucial that asylum seekers are permitted the right to work, both to promote self-reliance and to prevent problems of destitution such as ill-health, minor crime and prostitution (Refugee Action, 2006). In relation to removing NASS support for those who did not apply for asylum immediately on entry, as we note above, the UNHCR emphasise how the Border Agency must recognise that humanitarian difficulties faced by asylum seekers and their families may mean they are not able to acquire the right documents (2008: 11). According to Clements, in 2002 'more than two-thirds of the applicants to the United Kingdom ... failed to claim asylum at the point of entry and were thereby denied benefits' under this new clause (2007). In 2007 the Joint Committee on Human Rights drew attention to the impact of much of this legislation:

> by refusing permission for asylum-seekers to work and operating a system of support which results in widespread destitution, the treatment of asylum seekers in a number of cases breaches the

Article 3 ECHR threshold of inhuman and degrading treatment ... [it] falls below the requirements of the common law of humanity and international human rights law.

(JCHR, 2007: 110)

Increased Insecurity: Threat, Criminality and Terrorism

Another issue in the debate about asylum is the assertion that criminals and terrorists are being allowed to stay in the United Kingdom as asylum seekers, or that asylum seekers come to the United Kingdom and later commit criminal or terrorist acts. After the media focus on Sangatte, the terrorist attacks of 11 September 2001 also drove concern about border controls, and among other things, focused attention on the United Kingdom's migrant population, especially Muslims. New Labour's goal to reduce applications embodied the wide perception that the numbers of asylum seekers entering the United Kingdom were not only an economic burden, but also a post-9/11 security threat. Legal changes followed these events and the accompanying media coverage. As mentioned above, Blunkett underscored a concern that terrorists should not be able to seek the protections of the Geneva Convention or gain asylum (Blunkett, 2003).

Pressure also came from the United States. After the 7 and 21 July terrorist incidents in London in 2005, US diplomats accused the United Kingdom in a memo of allowing 'Londonistan' to develop by allowing terrorists to claim asylum (Hope and Blake, 2011). Beyond terrorism, fears of increased criminality were also contributing to a wider sense of concern in relation to asylum numbers. The claims of Chris Fox, president of the Association of Chief Police Officers (ACPO), that foreign criminals use asylum claims to travel around the world is one example (Thompson, 2003). New Labour was heavily attacked for bringing in the 1998 Human Rights Act, and it was colloquially referred to as a 'criminal's charter'. Its replacement with a UK Bill of Rights continues to be debated.

Alternative Perspectives

Refugee rights groups have drawn attention to a report by the ACPO which shows that statistically, asylum seekers are more likely than others to be the victims of crime, but no more likely to be perpetrators (2003, quoted in Refugee Action, 2012). Some commentators have criticised the links drawn between criminality or terrorism and asylum as both unfounded and irresponsible. As we note above, in April 2006 an UNHCR Report highlighted the danger that terrorism might be used to give legitimacy to efforts to bring in restrictive asylum and refugee controls (Campbell, 2006). The report argued that:

> This has led to a tendency to criminalise migrants, including asylum seekers, by associating them with people smugglers and traffickers ... the rise of xenophobia and fear of asylum seekers in many countries ... has led to a tendency to see refugees not as victims but as perpetrators of insecurity.
>
> (Campbell, 2006)

Both Prime Minister Blair's criticisms of hijackers being granted asylum, and Conservative leader David Cameron's desire to scrap the Human Rights Act, were criticised by Anthony Lester, the human rights lawyer and Liberal Democrat peer, who argued that 'The Human Rights Act was one of the first constitutional reforms of this government, but the Prime Minister persists in undermining public confidence in the rule of law and the protection of human rights by the senior judiciary' (quoted in Temko and Doward, 2006).

The 1951 UN Convention on Refugees, which defines the United Kingdom's obligations to people seeking asylum, actually gives an exception where that person 'has committed a crime against peace, a war crime, or a crime against humanity ... or a serious non-political crime' (UNHCR, 1951). Furthermore, Steve Symmons of the charity Asylum Aid has pointed out that 'Any seriously-minded terrorist is unlikely to choose a route where claiming asylum immediately puts you into contact with the authorities' (Ryan, 2003).

Increasing Deportations

From 1997 onwards, after New Labour came to power, as concern grew over 'abuse' of the asylum system, so did calls to deport more people whose cases had 'failed' and who might therefore be 'illegal immigrants' (Gibney, 2008: 154). Migration Watch believes that many asylum seekers are not genuine, and often advocates their detention and rapid removal following the rejection of a claim (Pallister, 2007). As mentioned above, in 2004 Michael Howard as opposition leader pushed for a withdrawal from the 1951 UN Convention. This would have enabled the refusal of all genuine refugees beyond a quota. Concern with removals became heightened with the growing sense of insecurity following 9/11, and Blair made it his priority to focus on deportations alongside his plan to reduce asylum applications (Milne and Travis, 2002). The issue of deportations was also raised in relation to criminality. This led to Blair's comment that there would be an automatic presumption that criminals should be deported, irrespective of whether the country they would be returned to was safe (see pp. 25–6).

Alternative Perspectives

As mentioned above, the number of deportations of 'failed' asylum seekers increased to 18,235 in 2006 (JCHR, 2007), and Blair celebrated this as an achievement (*Guardian*, 2006a). Despite the low proportion of rejected asylum claimants being deported during the 1980s, deportations were not raised then as an issue. The Labour Party in opposition maintained the stance that the Conservative government was too hard on immigrants, particularly refugees (Gibney, 2008). Gibney points out that the deportation gap – the difference between the number of people refused asylum and the number deported – became an issue only from 1997 onwards, after New Labour came to power (2008: 154). Historically, democratic countries have considered deportation 'a secondary instrument of migration control, one resorted to relatively rarely and with a degree of trepidation' because it is complicated to implement, and a traumatic and coercive use of state power over the individual (Gibney, 2008: 147). NGOs and refugee rights groups have expressed concern about the increasing moves to deport people more quickly, arguing that many cases could be genuine since many claims are rejected because of error. Suggested moves to withdraw from the Refugee Convention and send away genuine refugees were also fought by Refugee Council chief executive Maeve Sherlock, who called the plans 'dangerous, ill thought-out and hugely irresponsible' (BBC News, 2005). Liberal

Democrat chairman Matthew Taylor also said it was 'absolutely disgusting' (BBC News, 2005). The Refugee Convention states:

> The principle of *nonrefoulement* is so fundamental that no reservations or derogations may be made to it. It provides that no one shall expel or return (*'refouler'*) a refugee against his or her will, in any manner whatsoever, to a territory where he or she fears threats to life or freedom.
>
> (UNHCR, 1951)

The 'human rights' debate over deportation has been driven further by a small number of high-profile terrorism cases. For example, there have been repeated attempts since 2006 to deport the radical Muslim cleric Abu Qatada to face trial in Jordan. He has appealed in both British courts and the European Court in Strasbourg on the grounds that he would be tortured and subjected to an unfair trial if returned to Jordan. While Jordan promised otherwise, Amnesty International has warned against putting faith in this (*Guardian*, 2012a). Blair's intention to deport criminals to countries considered unsafe again raised the issue of withdrawal from the Human Rights Act and European Convention on Human Rights, since this could only be achieved through withdrawal. His conflict with the core *nonrefoulement* principle was identified in some of the press. For instance, the *Observer* reported that 'The article of the European convention under which [refugees] were originally allowed to stay – the Article Three anti-torture clause – *is one of only three which member states can abandon only if they leave the convention altogether'* (Temko and Doward, 2006). Regarding the concern about the Human Rights Act being a 'criminal's charter', a leader in the *Observer* claimed that there was a politically motivated tendency in 'the Blair government' to 'foster lies and bolster rightwing myths about its own Human Rights Act' (2006).

When the debate about the 'foreign criminals' case began to dominate the press, the focus on deporting 'failed asylum seekers' now began to be questioned from a different angle by the shadow minister for immigration, Damian Green. He argued that the government's controversial system had created a preoccupation which could have contributed to the Immigration and Nationality Directorate (IND) not deporting 'foreign criminals' (Press Association, 2006). Refugee rights groups and NGOs have argued that often it is the more visible asylum seekers, the ones who follow all the rules, who are targeted for deportation. It is important to remember that the debate about deportation concerns asylum seekers more widely, the vast majority of whom are law-abiding. It is often the high-profile 'criminal' cases that come to characterise the discussion, not the other cases of individuals who can easily be removed to drive up statistics. Maeve Sherlock, the Refugee Council chief executive, commented, 'The process of who gets removed and who doesn't can be very arbitrary. In too many cases the officials don't seem to chase the hardest cases but instead pick on people who co-operate with the authorities and play by the rules' (*Independent*, 2006).

The Benefits of Immigration

Political figures who refer to the benefits of general immigration to the United Kingdom most commonly mention its impact on the economy. An OECD 2006 assessment concluded that in fact migration had strengthened the UK economy. It stated that 'Record high inward migration has been adding to potential growth', and argued that 'international as well as UK evidence suggests that immigration can serve to make the labour market as a whole more fluid and wages less sensitive to demand fluctuations' (cited in Home Office, 2007). Multiculturalism and diversity are also mentioned in the debate as being beneficial and enriching British culture. For example, a *Guardian* editorial commented that 'The country's greatest strength lies in its diversity, its tolerance, and its respect for people of all faiths and cultures' (2005).

Alternative Perspectives

Clearly the widely held perspective explored above that immigrants and refugees constitute a burden to the country essentially excludes any discussion of benefits they might bring. Criticism tends to come from an evaluation of national interest. Migration Watch argues that the economic benefits of immigration are overestimated, and often this anti-immigration stance is conveyed in populist headlines and quotes. For example, the front page of the *Sun* claimed in 2007 that the economic benefits to the country of immigration were 'Equivalent to a Mars bar a Month' (Pallister, 2007). Multiculturalism has also been attacked. Shadow home secretary David Davis told the *Telegraph* in 2005 that 'Britain has pursued a policy of multiculturalism – allowing people of different cultures to settle without expecting them to integrate into society' (*Guardian*, 2005). David Blunkett in 2005 also adhered to the perspective that multiculturalism had failed, and launched 'citizenship' tests for immigrants to ensure their 'Britishness'. This was in turn criticised by Roger Hewitt from Goldsmiths College, who said that 'it seems, in fact, that far from being about to crumble, our multicultural society has come to develop strong roots' (*Guardian*, 2005).

Problems Faced by Asylum Seekers

Asylum seekers come to the United Kingdom (and other countries) because they are fleeing war or persecution. They might have been tortured or raped, and have certainly suffered great loss and upheaval. In addition, having moved very suddenly they usually face difficulty entering the United Kingdom because of their lack of documentation. If they are able to enter the United Kingdom, they are faced with distrust and great hardship. There is a well-documented lack of trust of refugees' narratives (see Daniel, 1995), and refugee rights groups point to the poverty faced by asylum seekers in the United Kingdom. Asylum seekers are not allowed to work, and the direct financial support (in the form of food and shelter vouchers) that the Border Agency provides to destitute asylum seekers amounts to less than income support, which is normally considered a minimum for survival (Faculty of Public Health, 2008). If an asylum application is not made as soon as an asylum seeker enters the country, the person might be refused support and accommodation. Concerns have also been raised about the standard of the care available, characterised by overcrowded detention centres whose management is contracted out to security firms like G4S. In one October 2012 example from a unit described as 'family friendly', the *Guardian* reported that 'unacceptable force' had been used by G4S security staff on 'A pregnant woman in a wheelchair [who] was tipped up and had her feet held ... as she was forcibly removed from the country' (2012d).

The Refugee Council has pointed out that:

Many asylum seekers have been through hugely traumatic circumstances in their home country and on their journey to the United
Kingdom, and arrive here with nothing. It is unacceptable to house
asylum seekers in sub-standard, unsecured and overcrowded conditions
for cost-cutting purposes while they seek safety here and wait for a
decision on their claim.

(Refugee Council, 23 March 2012)

In addition, many refugees suffer from post-traumatic stress, depres-
sion and mental health conditions as a result of torture and societal
upheaval, as well as physical health problems requiring greater
support (Faculty of Public Health, 2008).

Some of our interviewees suggested the main reason some genuine
asylum seekers seem inconsistent or untruthful is that they feel they
must adjust their story to something that is more likely to be believed
or that it is easier for them to talk about. For example, sometimes
women who have been raped do not want to speak of this. Also, if they
have done something that is considered illegal in their own country,
which would be judged harshly and might even receive the death
penalty (for example heavy criticism of the state), they might not be
willing to discuss it during the interview (refugee worker, Norwich).
Furthermore, given the large numbers of refusals of asylum, Refugee
Action points to:

a new and growing excluded class of people whose asylum applications
have been refused, who are afraid or unable to return to their countries
of origin, who have no contact with the authorities, no access to work
or mainstream support services, and little prospect of their situation
being resolved.

(Refugee Action, 2006: 2)

In theory refused asylum seekers are entitled to receive vouchers for
support, but they can only claim them if they agree to deportation to
their country of origin. Some feel their cases have been ill-judged and
fear persecution should they return home, so they are not willing to
accept this condition.

Recent research by Morag Gillespie of the Scottish Poverty
Information Unit has shown that 'Hundreds of failed asylum seekers
are living in Scotland on less than the UN's global poverty target of
77 pence ($1.25) a day', including pregnant women, disabled people

and children (Briggs, 2012). Gillespie called it a 'hidden crisis', and recommended that asylum seekers be allowed to work if they have been waiting six months or more for a decision (Briggs, 2012).

The Role of the West in Refugee Movements and Economic Forces in Migration

We noted above the importance of considering how the manner in which the global economy works contributes to forced migration issues, and the position of western capitalist economies and corporations as the beneficiaries of this economic system. Some commentators argue that because of the impact of colonialism and current foreign policies, countries such as the United Kingdom have particular responsibility to asylum seekers fleeing conflicts in which the country has been involved. They point out that many of the conflicts from which refugees are fleeing are 'directly attributable to the actions of the Western powers' (Hyland, 1999).

We have already detailed some of the ways in which western economic interests have contributed to global conflicts, for instance by financing corrupt leaderships in Africa and South America. We also observed how international conflicts are sustained by lucrative arms exports. All these western foreign policies contribute to conflicts that are causing the world refugee problem. The obvious recent examples of conflicts led by the West, in Afghanistan and Iraq, have driven large numbers of refugees to flee both into neighbouring countries like Pakistan and further, to seek asylum in the West. The 'war on terrorism' has driven US Defense Department spending and defence industry trade internationally. For example, in one Supplemental Appropriations Bill the US Administration requested over $1.1 billion in security assistance to fight terrorism in 45 countries. The 2002 Supplemental Appropriations Act included $387 million in 'foreign military financing', more than President Bush had requested (US Congress, 2002).

Maeve Sherlock from the Refugee Council in the United Kingdom noted that:

> richer countries like the UK are simply not pulling their weight when it comes to looking after people who are forced to flee their homelands.

The vast majority of refugees find help in developing countries, not the west, so we should be doing a lot more.

(quoted by Campbell, 2006)

Western economic imperatives are often criticised for contributing to or benefiting from the impoverishment of the developing world, leading to economic migration. Criticism of the World Bank and IMF for imposing 'conditionalities' based upon the 'Washington consensus' of economic liberalisation in exchange for loans was mentioned above (see Sahn, Dorosh and Younger, 1997). We also noted how this structural adjustment for developing countries results in increasing exports of what are often basic commodities and raw materials which yield low revenues. The prohibitive costs of technology combined with a lack of infrastructure mean that they continue to import higher-cost finished products from the West. Structural adjustment is argued to result in economic growth without a focus on sustainability, political stability and governance (Sahn et al., 1997).

We gave the example of Europe's common agricultural policy, which gives global advantage to European farmers through subsidies and support for environmental and rural development. However, this simultaneously prevents the developing world from competing globally. The environmental impact of large-scale fishing industries' technologically advanced trawlers and industrial long-line fishing is argued to have resulted in the decline of world fish stocks and damaged global fishing industries. Environmental disasters have always caused forced displacement of people, and they are increasing as a result of climate change and human-made destruction. The Refugee Convention does not offer protection for people displaced for such reasons, who are often just as vulnerable as political refugees, and who may have as great a need for refuge.

3

Media Content: Press and TV Samples, 2006

Our TV sample is drawn from news items on BBC1, BBC2, ITV and Channel 4, and the press sample is drawn from items in the *Daily Mail*, the *Daily Express*, the *Sun*, the *Mirror*, *The Times*, the *Guardian* and the *Telegraph*. We have focused on two key periods in which there was coverage of asylum and refugee issues, the first from 2006 and the second from 2011. The coverage was very intense during 2006, and we chose a period of three days following the resignation of Charles Clarke as Home Secretary in May of that year. We identified a series of themes and analysed news items using thematic analysis, noting the manner in which some themes were highlighted while others were downgraded. We were then able to assess whether the patterns of coverage we had identified occurred in our later sample of press and TV news items from 2011.

By 2011, the frequency and intensity of coverage had fallen in the press. In 2006, across the year as a whole there were 1,961 articles featuring asylum/refugees in our sampled newspapers; this reduced to 1,351 by 2011.[1] There was also considerable public interest in press coverage of controversial issues in the light of the Leveson Inquiry, and for these reasons we took a sample of one month for 2011. We have also, as far as possible, examined some of the trends in coverage for 2012.

---

1   Based on a search in the newspaper database 'newsbank' for the *Guardian*, the *Telegraph, The Times*, the *Sun*, the *Daily Mail*, the *Mirror* and the *Express*.

Case Studies of Media Content, 2006

Introduction to TV News Content

As noted, this first sample was taken from the period following Clarke's forced resignation on 5 May 2006. It had been revealed that foreign nationals had been freed from prison without being considered for deportation. Ten reports were drawn from 16, 17 and 18 May 2006, selected because they reflected a range of themes on coverage of migration and asylum, and key stories from the time. This sample included the early evening and late news bulletins for BBC1 and ITV (the most popular channels with the highest viewing figures), *Channel 4 News* and BBC2 *Newsnight*. BBC1 *Reporting Scotland* and BBC1 *Newsnight Scotland* were also included to enable some regional comparisons. We can see from the headlines how familiar themes in public discourse are reproduced. The issues of numbers, fraud, criminality and the sense of migration as a threat and a system in chaos are all present:

- 'Immigrant fraud' – BBC1 *Reporting Scotland*, 16 May 2006
- 'Illegal immigrants: now the prime minister admits he doesn't know how many are here' – BBC1 *6 O'Clock News*, 17 May 2006
- 'Tonight now the prime minister accepts he's failed on illegal immigrants' – BBC2 *Newsnight*, 17 May 2006
- 'A thousand foreign criminals released by mistake' – *Channel 4 News*, 16 May 2006
- 'The foreign criminals, illegal immigrants and human rights' – *Channel 4 News*, 17 May 2006
- 'Welcome to Britain where illegal immigrants are free to stay and work without fear of being caught' – ITV *Evening News*, 17 May 2006
- 'Is immigration an unstoppable force?' – BBC2 *Newsnight*, 18 May 2006
- 'Five Nigerian cleaners are in police custody' – *Channel 4 News*, 18 May 2006
- 'Five illegal immigrants arrested as they arrive for work at the government's Immigration Directorate' – BBC1 *10 O'Clock News*, 18 May 2006.

- 'On *Newsnight Scotland*: from migration to asylum' – BBC2 *Newsnight Scotland*, 18 May 2006.

Headlines Written by Focus Group Members

As part of this research we interviewed a series of focus groups composed of members of the public. We discuss the results from these in more detail later, but we can note one result here. At the beginning of each group session we asked the members to write a news headline from their own memory on the subject of refugees and asylum. They were almost all able to spontaneously reproduce headlines on exactly the themes seen in the above headlines, as the following examples demonstrate:

- '300,000 refugees in Britain', 200,000 missing
- Refugees taking over
- Crime rate increases in populated area: asylum
- More protests against volume of asylum seekers
- Britain being invaded
- Free homes for asylum seekers
- Refugees overflow
- 'Flood of refugees' from European countries
- Government putting more stringent laws on migration
- Asylum seekers taking our benefits
- More asylum seekers arrive from Afghanistan
- Britain allows more and more immigrants in
- Crack down on asylum seekers in hiding
- Migrants, how can we cope?
- Britain getting flooded by refugees
- Millions of homeless and vulnerable hit UK.

These headlines were written some years after the actual news headlines above had been released. It indicates how such coverage and its major themes imprint very deeply on public memory, although it does not follow from this that everyone necessarily believes what is said. It is noteworthy that only one of the headlines produced by the focus group members contains even a mention of the people arriving as being vulnerable.

Introduction to Newspaper Content

The newspaper sample from 2006 was also drawn from 16, 17 and 18 May 2006:[2]

- *Telegraph* (16 May 2006) 'Analysis: all we have to show after Blair's nine-year campaign for justice'
- *Telegraph* 1 (17 May 2006) 'Confessions of the removal man'
- *Telegraph* 2 (17 May 2006) 'The gentleman from Whitehall knows little'
- *Telegraph* 1 (18 May 2006) 'Commentary: it must be time for Labour to take the blame'
- *Telegraph* 2 (18 May 2006) '"A decade" to remove illegal migrants'
- *Mirror* 1 (17 May 2006) '"No point" chasing migrants'
- *Mirror* 2 (17 May 2006) 'Labour cock-ups no longer surprise us'
- *Mirror* 3 (17 May 2006) 'Migrants in "let off"'
- *The Times* 1 (17 May 2006) 'Immigration control a mockery'
- *The Times* 2 (17 May 2006) 'Officials "haven't the faintest idea" of immigrant count'
- *The Times* 1 (18 May 2006) 'Labour fails to shake off 50 years of vulnerability on immigration issues'
- *The Times* 2 (18 May 2006) 'A Reid agenda'
- *The Times* 3 (18 May 2006) 'The issues'
- *The Times* 4 (18 May 2006) 'We don't have a precise figure on this'
- *The Times* 5 (18 May 2006) 'Asylum seekers in the UK'
- *Express* (16 May 2006) 'An anti-British ideology that is just as sinister as the extreme right'
- *Express* 1 (17 May 2006) 'Revealed: how asylum seekers use your taxes to smuggle in relatives'

---

2 A Lexis Nexis search using the search terms 'asylum', 'refugee(s)', 'immigrant(s)' and 'immigration' produced 131 articles, a sample which was narrowed by selecting those articles that were most typical and related to the key stories of that period. We also excluded those articles that did not concern immigration to the United Kingdom. The final sample comprised 42 articles drawn from the *Sun* (7), the *Guardian* (5), the *Mirror* (4), the *Daily Mail* (6), *The Times* (8), the *Express* (6) and the *Telegraph* (6). Of these 34 discussed asylum seekers or asylum issues predominantly, or alongside economic migrants, and the data trends were drawn from this category unless otherwise stated (*Sun* – 4, *Mail* – 6, *Express* – 4, *The Times* – 7, *Telegraph* – 5, *Mirror* – 3, *Guardian* – 4).

- *Express* 2 (17 May 2006) 'Now we give up chasing illegals'
- *Express* 1 (18 May 2006) 'Blair and co haven't the faintest idea how to protect our shores'
- *Daily Mail* (16 May 2006) 'The drug godfather'
- *Daily Mail* 1 (17 May 2006) 'Haven't got the faintest! Civil servant in charge of deportations is asked how many illegal migrants there are in the UK. And his reply?'
- *Daily Mail* 2 (17 May 2006) 'Comment: wide open Britain: the shocking truth'
- *Daily Mail* 1 (18 May 2006) 'The Home Office is a mess say Reid's staff'
- *Daily Mail* 2 (18 May 2006) 'Deportations to take a decade says minister'
- *Daily Mail* 3 (18 May 2006) 'The lunatics are STILL in charge of the asylum; as ministers and civil servants admit they haven't a clue what's going on, the author of a devastating report on our immigration system says...'
- *Sun* 1 (17 May 2006) 'Lesbian faker win'
- *Sun* 2 (17 May 2006) 'Human right law will stay'
- Blunkett, D., *Sun* (17 May 2006) 'It's easy to cop out on illegals'
- *Sun* 3 (17 May 2006) 'We don't bother to hunt down illegals'
- *Guardian* (16 May 2006) 'Comment and debate: ignorant opposition: the prime minister is undermining public confidence in the rule of law and the judiciary'
- *Guardian* 1 (18 May 2006) 'Leading article: illegal immigration: removed from reality'
- *Guardian* 2 (18 May 2006) 'Comment and debate: diary'
- *Guardian* 3 (18 May 2006) 'Vast bulk of foreign prisoners to be deported after sentence, Blair says: political briefing: Department of Sin in a spin'
- *Guardian* 4 (18 May 2006) 'Asylum: asylum seeker injured in jump from second floor'.

Most of our data was drawn from this asylum seekers sample, but we considered other articles as evidence of the wider debate on the context of immigration. Only one article concentrated solely on a refugee:

- *Sun* (16 May 2006) 'Wheelchair don is jailed 22 years'.

And one concerned specifically economic migrants:

- *Sun* 4 (17 May 2006) '70,000 Poles in Scotland'.

A further seven articles either discussed 'immigrants', often without it being clear which type of migrant was being discussed, or referred to a story that concerned all groups of immigrants together, including asylum seekers and refugees:

- *Telegraph* 3 (18 May 2006) 'Big Brother immigration service is not the answer'
- *Mirror* (18 May 2006) 'I want all foreign prisoners deported (but that doesn't mean all); Blair's new pledge'
- *The Times* 6 (18 May 2006) 'We'll send prisoners back to "unsafe" countries, says Blair'
- *Express* 2 (18 May 2006) 'Rattled Blair gets a battering on the migrants we can't catch'
- *Express* 3 (18 May 2006) 'Close all our borders and end this immigration crisis'
- *Sun* (18 May 2006) 'PM sunk on exile 'em vow'
- *Guardian* 5 (18 May 2006) 'PM promises tough line on deportations'.

Who Speaks

We considered the range of voices included in the 34 articles that discussed asylum (or asylum alongside economic migration), and the position that these took on support, resources, or right to remain for the migrant group they were discussing (the groups were often conflated in the statements). Negative statements included phrases such as 'no right to be here', 'coming here for benefits, taking taxpayers' money' and 'we should be deporting more'. Of the total 99 statements recorded for quoted speakers, 42 were negative and critical, and just five speakers made statements that were supportive.

Statements and sources cited by the journalists in the articles were most commonly attributed to politicians (81 statements[3] across the

---

3   38 from the total of 81 politicians' statements recorded were critical of provision of support, resources or 'right to remain' in relation to those they were discussing, and two defended it.

34 articles in the sample of articles dealing with asylum or asylum and economic migration). Of these, 66 statements came from governmental politicians and authorities including civil servants, of which 24 were critical of provision of support. An example is the statement by Tony Blair regarding the 1,023 released prisoners who were not deported, that 'those people ... should be deported irrespective of any claim that they have that the country to which they are going back may not be safe' (*The Times* 2, 17 May 2006). Two expressed a positive position. The first came from Tony McNulty MP, who was quoted in *The Times* saying it may not be possible to deport 'foreign national prisoners' 'because of the parlous state of a particular country' (*The Times* 2, 17 May 2006). By implication he was acknowledging that they should be allowed to remain in the United Kingdom. In the other article, in the *Sun*, David Blunkett noted that 'if families are genuinely facing death and torture back home ... then we should treat them fairly and caringly'. In this example, however, Blunkett also stated that this group had declined in numbers, that support should be temporary, and he expressed a strong critical message about people he spoke of as 'illegals' (Blunkett, *Sun*, 17 May 2006). Of the 16 statements from politicians not belonging to the party of government, 14 were negative and none advocated the provision of support.[4]

Refugees and asylum seekers themselves made up just 3 per cent of the total number of included statements. These statements were only cited in an article in the *Express*, and were positive. There were two negative comments from anti-immigration think-tank Migration Watch, one in the *Express* and one in the *Daily Mail*.

Themes in the Coverage

In the content of the actual television and press news reports, we identified eight key themes in the coverage:

---

4 Only one statement was attributed to a human rights/refugee organisation, in the *Express*, and two statements were attributed to international authorities and governments, also in the *Express*. Lawyers and judges were quoted seven times: twice in the *Mail*, three times in the *Express* and once each in the *Sun* and *Guardian*. One of these statements asserted the migrants' rights. There were also three recorded statements from academics and other independent experts, two of which were critical of support, resources or 'right to remain' for the migrants they discussed.

- conflation of forced and economic migration
- numbers and exaggeration
- burden on welfare and job market
- criminality, threat, deportation and human rights
- the need for 'immigration control'
- the benefits of immigration
- problems facing asylum seekers
- global capitalism, imperialism and western responsibility.

We will discuss each of these in turn, and the role that they played in establishing specific meanings in the news texts.

Conflation of Forced and Economic Migration

On TV News

There was common usage of the term 'illegal immigrant' across national news reports, along with the derivative 'illegals'. Asylum seekers are therefore considered within debates about 'illegal immigration'.[5] Some of these programmes used the term 'illegal immigrant' in the headline, and only the Scottish regional broadcasts avoided the term altogether and consistently used the term 'refugees' when referring to asylum issues, despite the first of these programmes being about fraud in asylum claims (BBC1 *Reporting Scotland*, 16 May 2006; BBC2 *Newsnight Scotland*, 18 May 2006).

Much of the coverage was structured around the assumption that 'illegal immigration' is the result of 'abuse of' and 'problems in' the asylum system. As has been mentioned earlier, this is an explanation offered by the two main parties, and is reflected in public opinion in relation to asylum (Finney and Peach, 2005: 28). In the 17 May BBC2 *Newsnight*, the pejorative term 'illegals' was introduced into the debate by Sir Andrew Green of Migration Watch. A Home Office Minister was interviewed, and used the expression 'many of these illegals'. During the discussion the presenter asked 'why the government had failed to meet its target of removing more people than had failed

---

5 In the following broadcasts: BBC *6 O'Clock News* – 17 May 2006; ITV *Evening News* – 17 May 2006; *Channel 4 News* – 16 May 2006; *Channel 4 News* – 17 May 2006; BBC *Newsnight* – 17 May 2006; BBC *Newsnight* – 18 May 2006.

[asylum] claims'. The Minister commented that the solution to 'illegal immigration' lies in the asylum system, 'that goes precisely to Nick's point about getting the asylum system in order, which ... has been precisely what we're doing' (BBC2 *Newsnight*, 17 May 2006).

In the course of this interview, the studio backdrop showed Sangatte (a young man attempting to climb over a barbed-wire fence), often centred between the newscaster and the Minister. The Minister commented directly on this Sangatte footage, saying, 'the illegal population, such as it is, is multilayered and segmented, it's not just as the pictures behind you show those climbing over fences, very often it's those who come quite legitimately for six months'. The newscaster replied, 'Those are the visible ones' (17 May 2006). These 'visible ones' were actually from 2001, and were individuals who were potentially seeking asylum.

How many would claim asylum and how many would leave was a persistent theme in news reports. The ITV *Evening News* broadcast on 17 May, with its focus on 'foreign criminals' and 'illegal immigration', included the question asked to a Home Office official, 'How many people have claimed asylum since '97 and how many of these have left the country?' (ITV *Evening News*, 17 May 2006). There was no mention of how claims might be rejected erroneously. The Refugee Council has noted that 30 per cent of rejected cases are awarded refugee status on appeal (2010b).

Some coverage took the entry of people on overcrowded boats or hidden in the back of a lorry as absolute evidence that they were 'illegal immigrants'. This was evident in reports in the *Newsnight* of 18 May 2006 from South Africa and Spain. These were introduced by the newscaster as 'two countries calling for help to cope with *migrants who've arrived uninvited*' (BBC2 *Newsnight*, 18 May 2006 – our emphasis). It is inaccurate and misleading to refer to refugees as 'uninvited'. The Refugee Convention establishes the right for anyone to seek refuge anywhere in the world; it is a legally guaranteed invitation. In the report on Australia, the newscaster's first question regarding the automatic detention of asylum seekers referred to them inaccurately as 'unauthorised arrivals' when in fact the UNHCR guidelines and the terms of the Refugee Convention are clear to point out that refugees are always 'authorised' to enter a country and seek asylum (BBC2 *Newsnight*,

18 May 2006). The report from Spain claimed that 'Spain aims to *send most of these immigrants back home* but if no solution is found within 40 days they have to let them go.' This statement should not apply to refugees seeking asylum who cannot return to their homeland (BBC2 *Newsnight*, 18 May 2006 – emphasis ours).

Some coverage in this sample focused more specifically and critically on public debates around refugees and asylum. BBC2 *Newsnight Scotland* on 18 May opened with the statement that 'we take the debate on from those "seeking a better life" to those fleeing persecution'. The newscaster made the point that refugees seeking asylum are being conflated with economic migrants in the 'wider debate' on 'immigration'. She stated that forced migrants are not merely 'seeking a better life', a phrase actually used by a journalist in the BBC2 *Newsnight* broadcast that preceded this programme on the same night. The newscaster then gave viewers key information on the international protections that are legally accorded to refugees seeking asylum: 'under international law it looks like an open and shut case: if you fear persecution you can seek asylum in another country and if that fear is genuine you must be granted refugee status' (BBC2 *Newsnight Scotland*, 18 May 2006).

This presenter challenged the perspective in other media accounts, saying, 'Daily headlines reveal a different reality, *asylum seekers are being caught up in a wider debate from immigration to terrorism*' (BBC2 *Newsnight* Scotland, 18 May 2006 – our emphasis). Another journalist later in the programme also commented on the impacts on public understanding, noting that 'refugees and asylum seekers have become conflated in the public mind with economic migration, the non-deportation of foreign criminals and the so-called "war on terror"' (BBC2 *Newsnight Scotland*, 18 May 2006).

In the Press

In the press sample, issues of asylum were usually discussed alongside economic migration issues, very often without specifying different groups and using language such as 'illegal immigrants' to talk about both economic migrants and asylum seekers who have had their claims rejected. The term 'illegal immigrant' (or variations such as 'people living here illegally', 'illegals' or 'illegal population') was prevalent, appearing 90 times in 34 articles. The highest usage was found in the *Mail* (25), *The Times* (18), the *Telegraph* (13), the *Express* (7), the *Sun* (7) and the *Mirror* (7). There were many examples where this term was used to include asylum seekers and rejected asylum seekers, for example in the *Daily Mail*: 'illegal migrants, including an estimated 285,000 failed asylum seekers' (*Daily Mail* 1, 17 May 2006).

The *Guardian* also used the term 'illegal immigrant' 13 times. However, in one of these reports it criticised what it calls a 'rare but ... revealing slip' from Conservative Party leader David Cameron in the Commons, who referred to 'illegal asylum seekers' (*Guardian* 2, 18 May 2006). The *Guardian* called attention to this as 'an incendiary term much favoured by the smaller of our nation's newspapers', and even pointed out that it is 'a category of person that, in the authoritative view of the Refugee Council, cannot in fact exist' (*Guardian* 2, 18 May 2006). It is important to note that the *Guardian* articles that used the term 'illegal immigrant' often sought to debunk the alarmist accounts of 'floods' entering Britain, which accompanied use of this term in other papers. For example, one article in which nine uses of the term were recorded stated that:

> illegal immigration is a global phenomenon, affecting rich regions of north America and Europe as well as poorer ones like north Africa and central America ... published UK estimates of an illegal population of 480,000 mark us as a fairly typical north European country, not the world's illegal immigration honey-pot of the tabloid imagination.
>
> (*Guardian* 1, 18 May 2006)

As mentioned above, one common site of confusion is the way in which, according to the UNHCR, asylum seekers are often forced to arrive. The UNHCR says:

> UK immigration controls, much like many other states particularly in Europe, provide very limited legal channels for a refugee to enter in order to apply for recognition of their refugee status. As a result, most refugees seeking to enter the UK are forced to do so 'illegally', either using forged travel documents, or avoiding immigration controls altogether.
>
> (UNHCR, 2007)

Since refugees may flee suddenly and may not have any of their papers, they often cannot enter the country through the usual means. The Refugee Convention to which the United Kingdom has signed up recognises this, and states that countries must not penalise those arriving in ways that would normally be illegal. Yet the assumption is sometimes made, particularly in the press, that all people who enter the country without documentation, or covertly, are 'illegal immigrants'. Examples of this occurred five times in the 34 articles. In the *Daily Mail*, for instance, one editorial about 'illegal immigration' mentioned visa overstayers briefly before saying that the 'Home Office can give no accurate idea of how many failed asylum seekers are at large'. It asserted that 'These groups make up the vast majority of the illegal immigrants living here. Thousands also sneak in undetected each year in the back of lorries' (*Daily Mail* 2, 18 May 2006).

Another article in the *Telegraph* talked about 'clandestine entrants' along with 'failed asylum seekers' as being 'illegal immigrants' (*Telegraph* 1, 17 May 2006). In another article the *Daily Mail* discussed the report 'Welcome to the asylum' from 2001 (mentioned also in the BBC2 *Newsnight* broadcast, 17 May 2006), which stated:

> I watched one illegal immigrant cut his way through the canvas roof of a lorry. He stood on the tarmac, dazed but happy, and immediately claimed asylum. He did not mind being found; he knew he was in Britain for good.
>
> (*Daily Mail* 3, 18 May 2006)

The sense that asylum seekers were fraudulent was supported by language such as 'asylum cheats', 'frauds', 'bogus' asylum seekers and 'scamming' in twelve out of the 34 articles discussing asylum. For example, one article in the *Telegraph* argued that 'the surge in what became known as "bogus" asylum seeking and illegal immigration' began when travel became easier after the fall of the Berlin Wall (*Telegraph* 1,18 May 2006). The system was described as being 'abused' or 'exploited' five times in our sample. James Frayne from the Taxpayers Alliance was quoted in the *Express* saying, 'They have created a climate which encourages everyone to think they can get away with abusing the system' (*Express* 1, 17 May 2006). Some papers also highlighted particular cases of 'fraudulent' asylum, seeking to highlight what were seen as unjust incidences of people allowed to stay for human rights reasons because it had taken so long to assess their case, including the *Sun*'s article 'Lesbian faker win' (*Sun* 1, 17 May 2006). The *Express* used the phrase 'bogus asylum seekers' twice in one article discussing the deportation of rejected asylum seekers, and made the assumption that if their application was rejected this must mean that they were frauds. One such use was in criticism of the 1998 Human Rights Act (*Express* 1, 18 May 2006). The article stated that 'The Human Rights Act of 1998, which the Attorney General Lord Goldsmith absurdly regards as the Government's "greatest achievement" has in practice turned into a charter for foreign criminals, overstayers and *bogus asylum seekers*' (*Express* 1, 18 May 2006 – our emphasis).

This article also said that:

> Exposing the chronic incompetence of his own department, [Dave Roberts] went on to confess that he didn't have a clue how many *bogus asylum seekers* had been deported, nor how many overstaying foreign nationals had been told to leave the country.
>
> (*Express* 1, 18 May 2006 – our emphasis)

This theme of 'bogus' and 'fraudulent' claimants often supported calls for deportation of asylum seekers, which were found in twelve of the 34 articles that discussed asylum seekers or asylum and economic migration, and most often in the *Times* and the *Telegraph* (three times each).

Threatening Numbers

On TV News

The statistics used in these news reports were often unsourced, unclear and situated amongst superlatives and rhetoric.[6] Asylum applications had fallen from 84,132 in 2002 to 23,608 in 2006, a 72 per cent reduction (Blinder, 2011). But in the national media in 2006, much of the focus was on numbers of 'illegal immigrants'. The conflation of asylum issues with economic migration often coincided with and was

---

6 The regional programme *Newsnight Scotland* did, however, present sourced UN statistics that there are globally '9 million refugees', and when 'asylum seekers' and other 'displaced persons' are considered, 'that figure more than doubles' (18 May 2006).

included within the speculation over numbers of 'illegal immigrants'. In this period a key stimulus for coverage was a statement made by Tony Blair in the House of Commons, where he explained that 'There are no official estimates for the numbers of illegal immigrants into the United Kingdom. By its very nature illegal immigration is difficult to measure and any estimates would be highly speculative' (ITV *Evening News*, 17 May 2006).

The TV coverage then provided estimated figures for the 'real' number of illegal immigrants in the United Kingdom. ITV *Evening News* (17 May 2006) for example produced a statistic of '400,000 illegal immigrants', then extended the assertion that illegal immigrants are 'free to stay and free to work in the United Kingdom', though all those who enter are legally subject to immigration controls. There is little distinction here between people who are seeking asylum in the United Kingdom (whose claims might have been rejected despite their being genuine refugees) and economic immigrants. The use of 'alarmist statistics' in combination with the labelling of asylum seekers as 'illegal immigrants' was observed as a characteristic of coverage of Sangatte in the Cardiff Centre for Journalism study (Buchanan et al., 2003: 52). The Independent Race Monitor's Report has also criticised the focus on asylum numbers in the media, arguing that this encourages the belief that the numbers coming into the country are large (Coussey, 2005).

The BBC2 *Newsnight* programme on 17 May 2006 dedicated 16 minutes, including a report, a studio discussion and an interview with a Home Office Minister, to discussing numbers of 'illegal immigrants'. The report was introduced with the above statement from the Prime Minister that any 'estimates would be highly speculative'. The programme then attempted to speculate about possible 'numbers of illegal immigrants'. There was a report by a former immigration official, who cited an estimated figure commissioned by the government from Professor John Salt of University College London of 'half a million' illegal immigrants, based on the global numbers of 'illegal entrants'. John Reid was then shown stating the figure to be 'about 400,000'. Professor Salt has stated himself, however, that 'no country in the world' has an absolute figure (House of Lords, 2008). The former immigration officer attempted to enlarge Salt's estimate, adding 'two pools of migrants' because he claimed that the figure 'doesn't include all those not working nor dependants'. He thus increased the total figure to 1 million. He then argued that the United Kingdom presents various 'incentives' to migrants that would attract more than average, and justify a still-higher figure.

This speaker then asked for an estimate of 'illicit entry' from Harriet Sergeant (from the Centre for Policy Studies think tank), who produced a 2001 report on asylum 'after spending many weeks with immigration service staff' (BBC2 *Newsnight*, 17 May 2006). She then gave her own estimate as '300,000 people coming in just in Dover alone, but for the whole country we have no idea'. She made the extraordinary statement that 'any number of people can come into this country, nothing is stopping them' (BBC2 *Newsnight*, 17 May 2006). The former immigration officer then assured his audience – using language implying certainty – that 'either way you *have to conclude* that the total number of illegal migrants living in Britain today *has to be* in the millions, not the hundreds of thousands' (BBC2 *Newsnight*, 17 May 2006, our emphasis).

These conclusions set the tone of the studio discussion and the Home Office Minister's interview that followed the report. The newscaster took up this same issue with all three contributors, and several more caveats were given which acknowledged what the Prime Minister had said about the impossibility of determining numbers of 'illegal immigrants' in the United Kingdom.

> *Liberal Democrat leader Nick Clegg:* 'Well, since we don't know where they are, since we *don't know how many people there are*, it's extremely difficult to know what you do.'
> *Home Office Minister Tony McNulty:* 'I would say that *there's no official estimate*.'
> *Newscaster:* 'Yes, but none of us really knows *how many illegals*.'
> (BBC2 *Newsnight*, 17 May 2006 – our emphasis)

These are caveats within a wider discussion characterised by speculation about numbers. The newscaster went on both to cite figures ('hundreds of thousands or perhaps quarter of a million according to Sir Andrew Green') and to ask for them ('I'm asking you, what's your figure?'). The report, the studio debate and the interview with the Home Office Minister all presented the viewer with variable estimates and unqualified figures, with an overall sense of increasing numbers and the potential threat that these pose.

The BBC1 6 *O'Clock News* (17 May 2006) referred to numbers having 'ballooned', and stated that the Home Office struggled with the 'sheer scale of illegal immigration': claims not supported by figures. The *Newsnight* programme on 18 May 2006 was headlined 'Is immigration an *unstoppable force?*' (our emphasis). Such commentaries differ markedly from the tone of the *Guardian* article we noted above, and its conclusion that 'an illegal population of 480,000 mark[s] us as a fairly typical north European country' (18 May 2006,).

A vocabulary implying threat was also deployed with the imagery of natural disaster ('wave of Africans', 'flooding', 'staunching the flow'). Disaster rhetoric evokes people arriving in huge unmanageable numbers and implies an inherent danger, as in this example from BBC2 *Newsnight*:

> *Headline*: Is immigration an unstoppable force? And is it a force for good or ill?
> It's not just a row over the number of *illegal immigrants* in Britain, we're in Spain where a new wave of Africans is *flooding* to the Canary Islands into the EU, in America where George Bush is intent on *staunching* the flow of Mexican immigrants and in South Africa struggling with an *influx* of 2 million Zimbabweans. We'll be asking if anyone wants huddled masses any more.
> (BBC2 *Newsnight*, 18 May 2006 – our emphasis)

Images of George Bush and a US Border Patrol vehicle and uniformed officers further intensified this sense of threat. The language of 'natural disaster' is often used in this way to imply the 'threat' of illegal immigration, a phenomenon which was criticised by the Glasgow Media Group and subsequently by the Cardiff School of Journalism. Nonetheless, the BBC has failed to 'staunch the flow' (Philo and Beattie, 1999; McLaughlin, 1999; Buchanan et al., 2003).

BBC2 *Newsnight* on 18 May also discussed the historical scale of migration, and the newscaster spoke of 20th-century 'mass migration on an unprecedented scale'. This was actually contradicted in the first report on the programme, which argued that 'The last time the world experienced a global flux like this was in the decades before the First World War.' Robert Reich, the former US Labor Secretary, later said during the studio discussion that:

in about 1890 we had ...12 per cent of our population born outside the United States. Right now we have about 12 per cent of our population born outside the United States. In other words the great wave of immigration in the late 19th century is being replicated right now.

(BBC2 *Newsnight*, 18 May 2006)

Reich stated that the current level of migration was not unmanageable, that if 'we did it then, I think we can do it now'. There was no comment on this, but the newscaster did claim that of '191 million migrants' globally, 'more than half' came to 'just ten countries including the UK', implying that the 'burden' accepted by these ten was disproportionate, and including the United Kingdom in this. But of course if the United Kingdom was really taking one tenth of these migrants, then this would be over 9 million people. These figures are beyond even the views of Migration Watch.

Newsnight continued to pursue the issue of numbers and 'failed claims'. On the previous evening the newscaster had asked the Home Office minister, 'last year when we were dealing with the question why the government had failed to meet its target of removing more people than had failed claims .... Presumably those figures are now available. Have you met the target?' (BBC2 *Newsnight*, 17 May 2006). There was a focus on how many the United Kingdom could deport, and how quickly, rather than asking whether the United Kingdom should be deporting people to unsafe countries. The arguments about huge numbers of 'illegals' from a 'failing' asylum system lose credence when reports by the UNHCR are considered. It criticised the high number of refusals to grant refuge in the United Kingdom.

In the Press

The above themes were paralleled in the press. The statement by the Director of Border Control and Enforcement, Dave Roberts, that he had not 'the faintest idea' how many 'illegal immigrants' there were came to represent incompetence in the system. While the statement itself acknowledged a lack of figures available, it came implicitly to encompass the assumption that this unknown was an unmanageably large number. The statement featured in three headlines in our sample, but John Reid's observation that it was being 'caricatured' by the press was mentioned only by the *Telegraph* (*Telegraph* 1, 18 May 2006).

Of the 34 newspaper articles that discussed asylum issues or asylum alongside economic migration, eight used numbers and statistics with an undeclared origin. The *Telegraph* stated for instance that 'figures suggested last year there may be 480,000 illegal immigrants' without indicating where they came from (*Telegraph* 1, 17 May 2006). In another example in *The Times* there was a section of eight bullet points following the body of the text, where immigration statistics were given, all without source, including 'There are an estimated 310,000–570,000 illegal immigrants in the UK including more than 250,000 failed asylum seekers' (*The Times* 1, 17 May 2006). One *Express* article talked about a 'vast influx' of migrants, and used the phrase 'mass migration' three times (*Express* 1, 18 May 2006).

The *Telegraph* wrote of 'the surge in what became known as "bogus" asylum seeking and "illegal immigration" [which] began in the early 1990s', then gave rises in numbers, although asylum applications had actually fluctuated during the period. It commented on 'What had been a manageable trickle' becoming 'a cascade that the system struggled to deal with' (*Telegraph* 1, 18 May 2006). The *Mail* began one article by quoting the estimates from *Newsnight* the day before (BBC2 *Newsnight*, 17 May 2006):

> Immigration Minister Tony McNulty admitted last night that it could take ten years to deport all of the illegal migrants currently in the UK. He said the best estimate of the numbers here illegally, which was 'roughly in the ball park' was between 310,000 and 570,000.
>
> (*Daily Mail* 2, 18 May 2006)

The article went on to state that 'The admission came as a leading academic [Professor John Salt] claimed Ministers would not even begin to get a grip on the number of illegal immigrants hiding in the UK until at least 2014' (*Daily Mail* 2, 18 May 2006).

In this sample, as in the television coverage, we found 16 instances of language used to evoke 'natural disaster' in the articles that discussed asylum seekers: for instance they described migration being 'like an iceberg', 'swamped', 'soaring', 'waves', 'masses' and 'flooding in'. Eight of these 16 were in the *Express*.

A Burden on Welfare and the Job Market

On TV News

Programmes in the national sample made a point of mentioning economic incentives or draw factors that made countries like the United Kingdom more appealing. As we have indicated, such commentaries can conflate those seeking asylum with 'illegal immigrants'. The main focus of this coverage was on migration as a generic phenomenon, and did not include discussion of specific issues relating to refugees. For example, a journalist on *Newsnight* commented that 'Many illegal immigrants come to Spain from Africa because geographically speaking it's the closest European country, but their real goal is to reach France, Germany and Great Britain' (18 May 2006). The context of this within a wider discussion of economics and 'illegal immigrants' implied that their country 'choice' was economic, missing the relevance of refuge as a factor. Refugees may have no choice of country, and can be at the will of the agents they have paid to get them out of their country. However, refugees do often attempt to reach other European countries than the one they first enter. This is for many different reasons, such as colonial history which leads to people being familiar with the culture and language of their former colonising power.

The former immigration official on the *Newsnight* programme of 17 May argued that the United Kingdom presents various 'incentives' to migrants that would attract more 'illegal immigrants'. These 'magnets' included 'the international language of English' and 'migrant enclaves' that result from 'our Commonwealth history' (BBC2 *Newsnight*, 17 May 2006). The programme continued by listing other economic 'magnets' as on-screen bullet points, including 'US-style free labour laws ... EU-style generous welfare benefits' and 'A growing economy'.

In fact UK welfare benefits were and are relatively low by European standards. The United Kingdom had 'the largest proportion of persons living below the national poverty limit in 1994, only surpassed by Greece and Portugal' (Castles, Schlerup and Hansen, 2006). One study of asylum seekers found that 'Most respondents had very limited knowledge of what financial support they would be entitled to as asylum seekers or refugees in the UK' (Robinson and Segrott,

2002). And many expected to be self-sufficient: for example, a woman from Sri Lanka was quoted as saying, 'I thought you'd just go to a friend's house ... and find a small job and try to live a life' (Robinson and Segrott, 2002). Economic migrants in fact tend not to claim welfare because they work, and 'illegal' or 'undocumented migrants' cannot claim welfare benefits as this would make them known to the authorities. Rather than posing a burden, the OECD 2006 UK assessment concluded that in fact migration had benefited the British economy, adding to potential growth (Home Office, 2007).

In the Press

We found eleven articles which mentioned either jobs or welfare benefits critically, five of these occurring in the *Express*. Specific statements about the burden of immigrants on Britain occurred in five of the 34 articles discussing asylum seekers or asylum issues alongside economic migration, with three in the *Express*. Pejorative language also fed a theme of asylum seekers as a 'burden' in the *Express*. This included four uses of words such as 'pay-out', 'hand-out' and 'scrounger'. An article in the *Express* stated how Labour MP Frank Field 'has called for tax-paying British families to be given priority over asylum seekers when council flats are dished out' (16 May 2006). This *Express* article, which also referred to an 'overstayer' and Afghan hijackers in a discussion of asylum and migrants in general, argued that:

> Throughout Britain a fortune in taxpayers' money is being spent on giving free maternity care, HIV drugs and the rest to foreign 'health tourists' whose families have never put anything into the NHS pot. If this abuse is not stopped then the NHS a key marker of British civilisation will be doomed.... Yet staff are loath to withhold public services from these invaders.
>
> (*Daily Mail*, 16 May 2006)

In the *Daily Mail* article mentioned above, which describes a man claiming asylum as an 'illegal immigrant', an immigration officer is quoted saying, 'if we catch them, all we do is put them into the benefits system' (*Daily Mail* 3, 18 May 2006). It argues that 'in health, education and schooling, immigrants are in competition for scarce resources with the less well-off in British society' (*Daily Mail* 3,

18 May 2006). The article stated that 'British children find themselves increasingly in competition with 'Unaccompanied Asylum Seeking Children' [UASC] for help from social services'. The article went on to comment that:

> there is no limit on how many of these unaccompanied children can come in and claim services. This directly affects the level of care our most vulnerable children receive .... Westminster says its population of children in care has recently doubled due to UASC.
>
> (*Daily Mail* 3, 18 May 2006)

The article asserted that this was a political ploy by Labour politicians, who assumed that:

> unlimited immigration is, if not a benefit to the country, or even the traditional Labour voter, a benefit to the Labour Party .... Once they receive citizenship, new immigrants, [Tony Blair] obviously assumes, will be a huge source of Labour voters.
>
> (*Daily Mail* 3, 18 May 2006)

The headline of one *Express* article linked suggestions of a 'burden' on the country to increasing asylum numbers, and claimed that 'asylum seekers use your taxes to smuggle in relatives' (*Express* 1, 17 May 2006). The Taxpayers Alliance was quoted in the article saying politicians 'have created a climate which encourages everyone to think they can get away with abusing the system' (*Express* 1, 17 May 2006). In the article it revealed that asylum seekers are entitled to '£40 a week ... while their applications to stay are being processed' in addition to shared housing being provided. It stated that 'if they are granted refugee status the payout increases' to £60 income support along with 'other Government hand-outs', and that refugees are 'entitled to all the trappings of the welfare state' (*Express* 1, 17 May 2006). Where previously asylum seekers were entitled to a grant to help them settle in the United Kingdom, the Immigration, Asylum and Nationality Act 2006 meant they received an integration loan to be deducted from their benefits. The *Express* also did not acknowledge the level of proof required and difficulty of achieving refugee status, and the fact that the 2006 Act made applicants' status temporary. £60 is hardly enough to live on in Britain before deductions, yet the article claimed that this 'taxpayers' money' was being used to fund more asylum seekers' journeys to join relatives – despite the article stating that it took one Iranian man's entire £8,000 life savings just to get to Calais. None of the refugee accounts or quoted 'French security sources' in the article offered any evidence to support the claim that benefits were used to finance these asylum seeker journeys. Although families and friends in Britain were shown to provide some financial support, there was nothing to indicate that these were benefit claimants. The only reference implying this was a quote from Conservative MP Andrew Rosindell: 'This is something that will anger most law-abiding people. But it is yet another example of the Government's asylum system backfiring with the British taxpayer unwittingly funding something they are clearly against' (*Express* 1, 17 May 2006).

The Iranian man's account did bring into question the image portrayed above, that those who are granted refugee status live on 'government hand-outs', when he stated his ambition: 'I want to go to university and train to be a doctor or a vet' (*Express* 1, 17 May 2006).

Another *Express* article, focused primarily on rejected claimants, what it referred to as 'bogus asylum seekers' and 'illegal immigration', attacked the notion that migration could be of economic benefit to the United Kingdom. It argued that 'mass immigration' 'can never be a solution to economic difficulties', and speculated that while current migrants might be industrious, 'there is no evidence that their offspring, growing up in welfare Britain, will have the same outlook' (*Express* 1, 18 May 2006). In addition, it argued that economic migrants coming to work in Britain increase unemployment as they 'do the jobs that Britons will not', so 'an indulgent welfare system ... allows young people to sponge' in Britain (*Express* 1, 18 May 2006). It argued that 'mass immigration' also 'puts tremendous pressure on housing, the NHS, the roads and public services', and that in 'over-stretched Britain', 'we cannot take the strain anymore' (*Express* 1, 18 May 2006).

The Afghans who hijacked a plane and were permitted temporary leave to remain in the United Kingdom (they were attempting to escape from the Taliban and pleaded duress) were also targeted; the *Express* emphasised that 'British taxpayers' money' was used to provide for their accommodation, food and legal bills (16 May

2006). This theme of the financial burden on the state of 'terrorist' asylum seekers could also be seen in the *Express* following the 21 July bombings the previous year. The paper ran a story with the front-page headline 'Bombers are all sponging asylum seekers' (*Express*, 27 July 2005). James Curran has pointed out that although this accusation was later shown to be incorrect, 'it made a good cue to the poll, published in the same issue, inviting readers to answer the question: "Should all asylum seekers be turned back?"' (Curran, 2011: 17).

Criminality, Threat, Deportation and Human Rights

On TV News

The intense focus on a relatively small number of criminal cases also affects public understanding. As our focus groups show, the impact is to bundle together a wide range of diverse groups and people, including refugees, asylum seekers and other migrants, to produce an overwhelmingly negative perception. The reporting of individual cases leads to generalisations about groups. The term 'foreign criminals' is also used in this coverage in a way that conflates the categories of refugee, asylum seeker and undocumented migrant, as these are discussed under this label as one homogeneous group. The 1,023 'foreign criminals' frequently referred to in this coverage included 298 refugees and people seeking asylum (Clarke, 2006). All of the national TV reports, including *Channel 4 News* and BBC2 *Newsnight*, made direct use of the term 'foreign prisoners' or 'foreign criminals' in both headlines and reports, using language drawn from statements by politicians and government publications (e.g. House of Lords, 2006). This language groups together very different individual cases to justify blanket deportation. In contrast, the regional report from BBC1 *Reporting Scotland* (16 May 2006) with the headline 'Immigrant fraud', which concerned allegations of immigrants obtaining false passports, did not use this reductionist terminology.

In this debate, the human rights issue of deporting refugees back to countries in which they will be at risk of persecution is often unexplained. This can be seen in the following example from BBC1 *6 O'Clock News* from 17 May 2006, reporting on Prime Minister's Question Time in the House of Commons:

Prime Minister (Tony Blair): In the vast bulk of cases ... there will be an automatic presumption now to deport, and the vast bulk of people will indeed be deported. And those people in my view should be deported irrespective of any claim that they have that the country to which they're going back may not be safe.

Newscaster: So ... the prime minister making promises there but can he make them work?

Journalist: Not at the moment he can't, no, because judges have said that they believe that even someone [convicted] of a serious offence should have their human rights taken into consideration and that they perhaps should not be sent back to countries at which they'd be at risk. What Tony Blair is in effect saying is he needs to rewrite the law to say only if there is a specific, a personal, an individual threat to an individual could they be kept in this country. *They couldn't simply say, oh, I don't want to go to Iraq or Jamaica or Afghanistan or anywhere else 'cos I might get into a bit of trouble given what my track record is.* That means changing the law. He can't tell us yet how he'd change the law so there is still a big gap between the intention, the words and the actual legislation.

(BBC1 *6 O'Clock News*, 17 May 2006 – our emphasis)

The 'human rights' concern attributed to the 'judges' relates to people seeking asylum and refugees, but this was not explained. The journalist mentioned Iraq and Afghanistan, the countries of origin of some of the people seeking asylum, but did not reveal their refugee status. The human rights issue has been raised as these people if deported would be returned to war zones and countries where they are at risk of persecution. The journalist downplayed the risk by parodying the asylum seeker as making excuses – ''cos I might get into a bit of trouble given what my track record is'. It was also implied that in the current situation all someone needs to do is 'simply say' this to be allowed to stay, dismissing the harsh realities of an adversarial asylum process. It was stated that to tackle this Blair would need to make changes to 'actual legislation', but not what this would entail. The legislative change required would be the repeal of the UK 1998 Human Rights Act and withdrawal of the country's signatory status to the European Convention on Human Rights.

Gross and colleagues also studied broadcast coverage during May 2006, and discussed an earlier and concurrent story which featured during the dates we sampled. This focused on the case of the nine Afghan refugees who in 2003 had had their convictions overturned for the crime of hijacking a plane in 2000. The Home Office was continuing to attempt deportation in 2006, and Gross and colleagues argued that TV coverage of this was characterised by 'mug shots' and talk of 'hijacked planes'. They concluded that:

> Drained of its particularity, the story of the nine Afghan men, re-emerging in 2006 because of the culmination of an asylum case, actually comes to symbolise a series of threatening ideas associated with crime, terrorism and a risk to public safety through upholding human rights law.
>
> (Gross et al., 2007: 93)

In the Press

Of the 34 articles in the press sample which discussed asylum issues or asylum alongside economic migration, the discussion of crimes or harm inflicted occurred in five. The *Daily Mail*, for example, discussed 'The drug godfather', who it claimed 'controlled 90 per cent of Britain's heroin trade' (16 May 2006). Terrorism was also discussed in three articles, and nine articles covered the deportation of criminals or terrorists. Examples included Lord Falconer's statement regarding deportation that 'If members of the public are put at real risk by the release of a prisoner, then that risk does not go away because of the offender's human rights' (*Sun* 2, 17 May 2006). One article which discussed an individual refugee highlighted the criminal case of 'The wheelchair don', claiming that 'It is suspected that over the years 25 people were murdered in connection to his rackets' – and pointed to demands for an 'inquiry into how the mafia boss, believed to have come to the UK in 1997, was granted refugee status' (*Sun*, 18 May 2006).

The terms 'foreign prisoners' and 'foreign criminals' were used 17 times in the 34 articles which discussed asylum seekers or asylum and economic migration; five of these were in the *Express*. One example in the *Daily Mail* on 17 May described the Immigration and Nationality Directorate as 'reeling from the foreign prisoner release scandal' (*Daily Mail* 1, 17 May 2006). The *Daily Mail* also concluded another article from 17 May with the question, 'Is it surprising that the Home Office already shell-shocked by the scandal of the freed foreign prisoners now seems to be in melt-down?' (*Daily Mail* 2, 17 May 2006).

The following day an article in the *Daily Mail* entitled 'The Home Office is a mess, say Reid's staff' identified what it referred to as a 'chronic failure' in the department and in immigration control. The report concluded that 'its agencies have failed to protect the public' (*Daily Mail* 1, 18 May 2006), though it provided no examples.

The deportation of criminals was intrinsically linked to debate about the Human Rights Act, which is sometimes referred to as a 'criminal's charter', a term used once in the *Express*. Six articles (out of the 34) made direct attacks on the European Court of Human Rights or the Human Rights Act. By contrast one article in the *Guardian* detailed the benefits of these legal measures at length, describing them as protecting 'the civil and political rights of everyone, not just minorities'. It criticised Cameron's Conservatives and the *Sun* alongside Blair's position and previous threats to weaken the Act (*Guardian*, 16 May 2006). It argued that the criticism of the decision made regarding the Afghan hijackers came 'without reading the judge's reasons and before the Home Office had decided whether to appeal' (*Guardian*, 16 May 2006).

'Failed' asylum seekers who had committed no crime were described as being 'at large' by David Davis in the *Daily Mail*: 'It is hard to believe the Home Office is in a position to assess the threat to the public safety of every single one of 250,000 failed asylum seekers currently still at large in the UK' (*Daily Mail* 1, 17 May 2006). The phrase was adopted four times by journalists elsewhere, sometimes alongside the phrase 'illegal immigrants' instead of 'failed asylum seekers'. The phrase 'at large', normally only used in relation to escaped criminals, was found four times in the *Daily Mail* and once in the *Express*. Another article for instance stated that 'the Home Office can give no accurate idea of how many failed asylum seekers are at large' (*Daily Mail* 2, 18 May 2006). In the *Express*, in an attack on the BBC coverage of Africa, it was argued that 'brutality, corruption and a thirst for civil war' are causes of emigration from that continent, and that they 'arise out of African tribal culture' (16 May 2006). This view of African 'tribal culture' does not recognise the diversity across the African continent, between different cultures, histories and political systems in over 50 states. In addition, what is missing from such narratives is the contribution made by outside powers and the developed world to the conflicts that have developed. This includes for example the promotion of ethnic difference by colonial powers in Rwanda, the instigation of conflict as a way of fighting the cold war in Angola, and the exploitation of natural resources for the developed world which has financed conflict, as in the Democratic Republic of (DR) Congo. Such analysis is missing from accounts that focus simply on images of 'tribal fighting', and which derive from postcolonial assumptions about what Africans are like.

The *Express* was also very critical of what it saw as the undermining of British identity, arguing that with a 'neurotic loathing for Britain's heritage' the Labour Government 'has used mass immigration as a weapon to transform the country into a multicultural society' (*Express* 1, 18 May 2006). In an article that discussed 'failed' asylum seekers alongside economic migrants, it noted that 'Ministers prefer to hector us about discrimination [rather] than to clamp down on asylum abuses.' The article criticised Labour's 'leftwing government', comparing it to Soviet-era communism. It stated that:

> We cannot take the strain anymore. But rather than restoring border controls, Blair is now stressing the need for identity cards. That will do nothing to solve the crisis. If the Government cannot keep track of foreign criminals and has allowed our benefit system to be abused by gangsters, then an ID national register will only worsen the problem. A regime that has shown such contempt for British identity has no right to lecture us on how to protect our identities.
>
> (*Express* 1, 18 May 2006)

This article underscored a theme established in an earlier *Express* article criticising what it called 'internationalist extremism', describing this in a headline as 'An anti-British Ideology that is just as sinister as the Extreme Right' (16 May 2006). This ideology, it was argued, is 'based on the denial that we owe any special obligations to our countrymen' (*Express*, 16 May 2006). The *Express* took as evidence the Afghan hijacker case, saying that this was 'a classic act of internationalist extremism; the interests of British people being over-ridden time and again' (*Express*, 16 May 2006).

ICAR has argued that there is an assumption underlying the public discourse that criminals who are 'foreigners' are somehow worse than British criminals, and highlighted the different language used to describe the two groups (2011). For example, in a discussion of the issue of foreign national offenders in the House of Commons on 22 June 2010, they were described as 'nasty people' three times (Hansard, 2010). It is interesting to note as a counterpoint to the coverage in our 2006 sample, the outcome of the case of two of the group of foreign nationals who featured so prominently in the tabloids. They subsequently won a Supreme Court decision to grant them damages for unlawful detention.[7] One of the justices who ruled on the case was Lord Collins, who in his speech quoted the Magna Carta (1215) from Lord Bingham's book *The Rule of Law*: 'no free man shall be seized or imprisoned ... except ... by the law of the land' (quoted in Webber, 2011). The Institute of Race Relations (IRR) detailed the personal impact this media 'scandal' had on these individuals, one of whom was Walumba Lumba from DR Congo. According to IRR he:

> should have been released in June 2006 at the end of his four-year sentence for wounding – but he remained in prison for over four and a half years, under Immigration Act powers, which set no statutory limit on immigration detention. His marriage broke down, he began to suffer psychiatric problems and eventually, in February 2011, he left the UK 'voluntarily' rather than remain locked up.
>
> (Webber, 2011)

Need for 'Immigration Control'

On TV News

The coverage on this issue again emphasised the sense of crisis. On the ITV *Early Evening News*, a journalist reporting live from the House of Commons lobby suggested that there was poor immigration control and 'another day of immigration chaos' (17 May 2006). This was reinforced by a banner headline which read 'Immigration chaos?' – a question that became a statement of fact when the reporter concluded that the immigration service was 'a system that I think genuinely is in chaos'. He made the argument that the 'immigration chaos' was caused by a lack of immigration control, suggested that 'people watching ... will be profoundly disturbed' by this, and lamented 'how little knowledge we have about what's really going on'.

---

7   See: http://www.supremecourt.gov.uk/docs/UKSC_2010_0062_Judgment.pdf

He did, however, also make the point that 'illegal migrants' should not be demonised, noting that 'most of them work quite quietly without causing any trouble, and eventually enter the legitimate system' (ITV *Early Evening News*, 17 May 2006).

Channel 4 News on 17 May 2006 extended the idea of immigration being 'out of control' to the whole of the Home Office. The newscaster's introduction to the broadcast asked, 'can the government *regain control* over the Home Office and sort out the mess, or are the Tories right: they're simply rattled?' (*Channel 4 News*, 17 May 2006, our emphasis). The shadow immigration minister who was interviewed next linked this statement directly to a criticism of Labour, addressing the newscaster informally:

> You've been a journalist for a long time and you don't remember covering these stories ten years ago because these sort of stories weren't about... over the past few years we have completely lost control in this country of our borders.
>
> (*Channel 4 News*, 17 May 2006)

The shadow minister then gave examples of 'controls' he claimed had been 'lost' – 'the embarkation controls, controls of people going out of the country so that's why we don't know who's here' – and sketched threatening implications for the United Kingdom: 'criminal gangs, people traffickers know that Britain is a soft touch and that's why we've become the centre for people working even at the heart of government where you might think the security checks were pretty stringent' (*Channel 4 News*, 17 May 2006).

This claim of serious crime was associated with the case of five contract cleaners found working in the Home Office without correct documentation, to argue that the immigration control problem went to the 'heart of government'. The case of the 'illegal immigrant' cleaners is interesting in that it illustrates how some TV news programmes can move into the language and perspective of the tabloids to which they are supposed to be providing an alternative. 'You couldn't make it up', said the Conservative shadow minister, 'I said that, that was my line,' said the newscaster, although it is actually a favourite phrase associated with a *Daily Mail* columnist. The Channel 4 reporter on the story stated that 'the very people they were supposed to *kick out of the country* had been hired to clean their desks' (*Channel 4 News*, 17 May 2006, our emphasis).

In the Press

The need for 'immigration control' was a theme arising in just over half (19 out of 34) of the press articles discussing asylum seekers or asylum alongside economic migration in our sample from 2006.[8] References to a system in 'chaos' and similar terms (such as 'shambles', 'mockery' and 'fiasco') were found 24 times in these 2006 articles discussing asylum or asylum issues with economic migration issues, including eight mentions in the *Daily Mail* and seven in the *Express*. The word 'mockery' appeared repeatedly in the sample, as for example when Labour MP David Winnick described Dave Roberts' statement as illustrating 'a mockery of the immigration control system' (*Telegraph* 1, 17 May 2006). The *Sun* responded to the same statement, saying, 'His astonishing revelation will heap even more pressure on the Government over its shambolic immigration policy' (*Sun* 3, 17 May 2006).

The United Kingdom was described as having 'doors open' or being a 'soft touch' four times. A *Daily Mail* comment section was resolutely headed 'Wide open Britain: the shaming truth'. It described 'chaos in the Home Office', and stated that Tony Blair had 'lost all control of Britain's borders' (*Daily Mail* 2, 17 May 2006). An article by David Blunkett stated that 'if we say they can receive benefits and housing for ever, then anyone who touches our soil will be here for eternity, supported by the rest of us. And tens of millions round the world will get the "soft touch" message' (Blunkett, *Sun*, 17 May 2006).

In another article that day, Dave Roberts was referred to as exposing 'the hopeless inadequacy of the asylum system', and it was stated that 'Labour Committee members accused the official of making a "mockery of the immigration control system"' (*Daily Mail* 1, 17 May 2006). A quotation from Migration Watch's Sir Anthony Green formed the concluding remark in the article, that the 'Home Office has given up on enforcing any effective control of foreigners who come to Britain, illegal or otherwise' (*Daily Mail* 1, 17 May 2006).

---

8   These were mainly in *The Times* (5), the *Express* (4) and the *Daily Mail* (4).

The issue of immigration control was often linked to a concern that 'Britain takes too many', and in one *Express* article Conservative MP Tony Rosindell stated that 'The only reason they press to come to Britain is because we are a soft touch. It's time that changed' (*Express* 1, 17 May 2006).

The Benefits of Immigration

On TV News

In the national news programmes discussed here, many of the positive statements were conflated with negative issues that dominated programme content or with negative language. There were few instances of benefits being attributed specifically to asylum seekers or refugees, and most references were to 'immigrants' in general. Positive factors raised included:

- benefits to a host country's economy (primary category)
- cultural enrichment
- contribution to home societies and remittance income.

References made in the national news sample to the benefits of migration were minimal in the context of the wider picture being presented, of 'vast' numbers of 'illegal immigrants'. The benefits of migration were raised in studio discussions, or as caveats, rather than as a theme structuring the programme. One example using the first two 'benefits' comes from Damian Green, then shadow immigration minister and now Immigration Minister for the Coalition, who stated that 'I think Britain has benefited both economically and culturally from immigration' (*BBC2 Newsnight*, 18 May 2006). The newscaster questioned the contradiction between his comments about the benefits of migration and his arguing in favour of strict limits on immigration. She said, 'you want to control immigration, but you need immigration, but culturally you don't think immigration necessarily works?'

The same shadow minister also made this point on *Channel 4 News* on 18 May 2006: 'We welcome immigration; we think immigration is good for the economy and the Conservative party welcomes modern Britain which has been enriched culturally as well as economically by immigration.' He then returned to the issue of immigration control, and an apparent need to deport 'illegal immigrants', saying, 'We need people who come here legally to work or to study, we need to know who's here and we need to know that those who should not be here can be traced by authorities and can be deported' (*Channel 4 News*, 18 May 2006).

Where economic benefits were discussed more specifically, these related either to migrants doing undesirable unskilled jobs, or to their being highly skilled professionals. An example of the first category was made by Lord (Tom) McNally, as the Liberal Democrat speaker on home affairs:

> These people aren't organised criminals as sometimes our tabloids would like us to think – that everyone that's an illegal immigrant must be in organised crime – the vast majority are poor people looking for work and making a contribution to our economy by doing dirty jobs.
> (*Channel 4 News*, 18 May 2006)

His stance was sympathetic, and offered an indication of the possibilities of balance in other media depictions which focus on migrants as threatening or as criminals.

The inclusion of an African migrant perspective made a significant difference in terms of balance in the BBC2 *Newsnight* coverage on 18 May 2006. The guest, Sorious Samara, was a filmmaker who describes himself as an 'immigrant'. He reinforced the issue of benefits to host countries from migration, and gave a factual example of highly skilled migrants, 'nurses and doctors ... who come here are already trained'. Samara also made a point relating to cultural enrichment, stating that in both the United Kingdom and the United States the 'migrant' contribution is embedded into the essential structures and social fabric of the countries and is fundamental to what are historically 'diverse cultures'.

Another programme that successfully combined discussion of 'benefits' of refugees to the host country with comments on the problematic context of their migration was the regional BBC1 *Newsnight Scotland* broadcast on 18 May. The programme attributed benefits directly to refugees, not just immigrants. Ken McDonald presented the viewer with a list of the internationally famous: 'Albert Einstein, Madeline Albright, Casanova, Chopin, Victor Hugo, Béla Bartók, Peter

Lorre, President Thabo Mbeki, all in their time were refugees. Today at this integration project in Glasgow these are their Scottish counterparts' (18 May 2006). This put recognisable and respected faces to the notion of refugees benefiting society. The programme then introduced three women seeking asylum who gave their own stories, 'Scottish counterparts' of the famous refugees. It thus accorded the women a high level of respect, and recognised their potential as citizens.

In the Press

The benefits of immigration were a marginal theme, mentioned directly in just one of the 34 articles discussing asylum seekers or asylum alongside economic migration in the 2006 press sample. This *Daily Mail* article stated that immigration benefits only the middle class: '[It] has raised our standard of living and allowed us to enjoy service industries previously out of reach. Domestic help, builders, minicab drivers and car-washers are all half the price of the British equivalents – if you can find one' (*Daily Mail* 3, 18 May 2006).

While the article allowed that these economic migrants had benefited the country, it was highly critical of asylum, which was presented as a burden. We also found one article that discussed solely economic migration, which was sympathetic and concerned the '70,000 Poles in Scotland'. In this article, a large employer was quoted as saying, 'I like working with them. They are hard-working and reliable.' This was followed by the accounts of five Polish workers who described the improvement their coming to the United Kingdom had brought to their lives (*Sun* 4, 17 May 2006).

Problems facing Asylum Seekers

On TV News

The regional *Newsnight Scotland* dedicated a whole programme to this issue. This programme also included visual illustrations of opposition to UK government policy. Images of detention centre protests began a report in which there was representation of three NGOs supporting refugees seeking asylum. Further images of a protest outside Dungavel detention centre included a close-up of men looking out of a window, illustrative of the confinement of people seeking asylum in the United Kingdom. Footage of protest indicated both that the government policy of detention was actively contested and that asylum seekers receive some public support. Footage of the demonstration showed the crowd as multi-racial, including children, with visible placards, featuring statements such as 'ASYLUM SEEKERS WELCOME' (18 May 2006).

The programme also showed women and the families of refugees, which is significant given that up to 80 per cent of refugees are women, but their voices are rarely heard (UNHCR, 2002). Previous research has shown that the exclusion of women and children seeking asylum from both television and press coverage of refugee and asylum issues is often the result of inadequate time to research or explore an issue that requires sensitivity and patience. (It is believed that a high proportion of female refugees have been raped: Buchanan et al., 2003: 34–5.) The women's accounts of their experiences seeking asylum humanises them and gave agency to them. They were able to tell how they actively escaped in order to protect themselves and their children. Their contribution was important in informing viewers of the very different circumstances of those seeking asylum. The women gave their reasons for seeking asylum: 'war in Ethiopia' and 'they wanted to circumcise me and my daughter'. One stated that she was 'forced to come in this country' (BBC1 *Newsnight Scotland*, 18 May 2006). The Cardiff School of Journalism's research also found that the media were primarily relying on official sources such as government and police chiefs, with little space being given to the refugee voice even via NGOs or refugee support groups (Buchanan et al., 2003).

The *Channel 4 News* broadcast from 18 May 2006 included the chief executive of the Immigration Advisory Service, Keith Best, as a guest who confronted the issue of asylum seekers being denied the right to work. When the newscaster asked him whether there were 'illegal immigrants probably in every government department', Best flagged up the distinction between asylum seekers and other migrants:

> I don't know if these people were failed asylum seekers or not, but why doesn't the government allow asylum seekers to work, for example? It's an act of vindictiveness which really bears no deterrent validity whatsoever and stops people contributing to the economy.
>
> (*Channel 4 News*, 18 May 2006)

The *Newsnight* broadcast from 18 May offered a vivid depiction of 'immigration controls' in Australia. The programme spoke of the government's 'tough talk' and 'no-nonsense approach', demonstrating that 'outback detention centres were used to incarcerate thousands of asylum seekers' whom the government 'considered to be queue jumpers'. Reference to refugees as 'queue jumpers' implies they are somehow behaving illicitly, although the actual policy was to detain automatically anyone seeking asylum 'without a visa' (*Newsnight*, 18 May 2006). It was not pointed out that different laws and protections apply for refugees.

The physical impact of the Australian government's 'tough talk' was examined. This government's policies were far more than mere talk, as the images in the report itself revealed. They showed very young children being incarcerated behind 20 ft high razor-wire fences in a vast, heavily fortified detention centre. The policies and detention centres were not critically questioned in the programme, although there was criticism of the overall migration policy. International pressure ultimately led to the closure of the 'outback detention centres' (see, for example, *Guardian*, 2006b, 2007). The Australian editor of *Guardian Weekly*, Natalie Bennett, has cited 'horrific, inhuman treatment of refugees and asylum seekers' as one of the reasons she left Australia (Bennett, 2007). These problems of policy were not raised by the presenter, but there was an account of the global problems generated by migration and their impact on poor countries. A reporter noted for example that there are more Malawian doctors in Manchester than in Malawi, and that more nurses migrate from Malawi than are trained there each year. Australia was criticised for behaving like a big company 'recruiting workers it needs and rejecting those it doesn't', and by the newscaster for wanting only 'the cream of the crop' and 'not contributing to a better globalisation' (*Newsnight*, 18 May 2006).

In the Press

Discussion of the problems facing asylum seekers was usually a minor theme, and occurred in only three of the 34 articles discussing asylum or asylum and economic migration, twice in *The Times* and once in the *Guardian*. This included an article about a 'failed' asylum seeker who attempted suicide by throwing himself from the second-floor landing of a detention centre out of fear of being returned to Afghanistan after awaiting removal for a year. It mentioned that 'Two other detainees are believed to have injured themselves in similar incidents and a third man is said to have cut his stomach and chest to protest against conditions at the centre' (*Guardian* 4, 18 May 2006). *The Times* stated that 'Although it is now de rigueur to highlight the contribution made by immigrants, it is worth remembering the hostility that greeted the West Indians' who arrived on the *Empire Windrush* in the 1950s (*The Times* 1, 18 May 2006). There was another brief mention in another *Times* article, acknowledging that it was 'a series of unfortunate overseas events, notably strife in Kosovo' that 'sent waves of desperate people in Britain's direction' (*The Times* 2, 18 May 2006). The *Mirror* included a story on this 'hardship' theme in its Irish edition, which concerned the hunger strike of 41 Afghan men appealing against the rejection of their asylum claims, of whom seven had been hospitalised (17 May 2006).

The Role of the West in Refugee Movements
and Economic Forces in Migration

On TV News

These issues were rarely discussed or mentioned in any of the coverage we have examined. One issue of BBC1 *Newsnight Scotland* did raise the issue of asylum in terms of western responsibility, and began by informing viewers that 'refugee organisations from across Europe' are 'calling on EU countries to end inconsistent treatment of refugees', prompting the question of whether they can 'agree on a Europe-wide policy for those fleeing persecution' (BBC1 *Newsnight Scotland*, 18 May 2006). Rather than presenting the refugees themselves as a problem, the programme drew attention to the inconsistencies in European countries' current treatment of refugees. The studio introduction made an important distinction between migration and forced migration. The full explanation and sourcing of the legal definition of a refugee seeking asylum was then presented by a journalist: 'Under international law a refugee is a person with a well founded fear of persecution and they must be granted asylum' (BBC1

Newsnight Scotland, 18 May 2006). This stressed the legal responsibility of western countries to grant this right. The explanation of legal protections granted to refugees was represented visually by a studio backdrop image of a young African woman holding a baby, with yellow European stars superimposed. A Scottish Refugee Council NGO representative also informed viewers about how the Refugee Convention is based on legal and moral imperatives established 'in the 1950s ... in the wake of the Second World War and in recognition of the fact that millions of Jews who perished in Nazi Germany were actually denied access to safety in European countries' (*Newsnight Scotland*, 18 May 2006).

In the Press

The notion of the responsibilities of western countries was mentioned once in the press sample, in criticism of what was seen as the BBC's stance on this. The *Express* claimed that the BBC 'scour the African continent in search of dying children' out of determination to 'make the British people responsible for the plight of a vast continent' (*Express*, 16 May 2006).

We now move on to examine our 2011 sample, and will be able to make some comparisons between the two periods.

4

Case Studies of Media Content, 2011

Introduction to TV News Content

The second qualitative television sample was taken from June 2011, the period when the government backlog in asylum cases, announced in 2006, was cleared. A Home Affairs Select Committee Report criticised the way this was done, likening it to an 'amnesty' for asylum seekers. A new removal centre was also opened during this period, Morton Hall in Lincolnshire. All the asylum-related broadcasts occurred on one day during that week, 2 June 2011. Five reports were drawn from this week, selected because they reflected a range of themes on coverage of asylum, and the key stories from the time. We examined the lunchtime, early evening and late news bulletins for BBC1, BBC2, ITV and *Channel 4 News*, and found the following programmes concerning asylum:

- *Channel 4 News*, 2 June 2011 – 'Now, the government has denied there is an unofficial amnesty...'
- ITV *News at Ten*, 2 June 2011 – 'An amnesty in all but name, how thousands of asylum seekers remain in Britain, unchallenged and unchecked'
- ITV *Lunchtime News*, 2 June 2011 – 'MPs are warning 160,000 asylum seekers are being allowed to remain in the UK to clear a large backlog of claims totalling nearly half a million'
- BBC1 *Lunchtime News*, 2 June 2011 – 'Soft on immigration – the government is accused of allowing so many asylum seekers into the country that it amounts to an amnesty'

- BBC1 *10 O'Clock News*, 2 June 2011 – 'How hundreds of thousands of asylum seekers have been allowed to stay in the UK. MPs say it amounts to an amnesty.'

Introduction to Newspaper Content

The June 2011 newspaper sample was drawn from the same period as the TV news above.[1] The following are the articles that formed the main sample, which all discussed asylum issues or asylum alongside economic migration:

- *Daily Mail* 1 (2 June 2011) 'Lawns with Greek statues, a computer suite, hairdressing lessons … inside our newest holding centre for migrants'
- *Daily Mail* 2 (2 June 2011) 'Asylum 'amnesty' lets thousands stay in UK'
- *Daily Mail* 1 (3 June 2011) 'Amnesty shambles lets in 250,000 asylum seekers'
- *Daily Mail* 2 (3 June 2011) '*Daily Mail* Comment: Tories must end this immigration fiasco'
- *Daily Mail* (6 June 2011) 'This Zimbabwe policeman is denied asylum in Britain …. But Mugabe torturer can stay'

---

1   Articles were selected again using Lexis Nexis. This led to a total number of 848 articles, and this sample was narrowed by focusing in on articles discussing key events and stories from that month. We also excluded those articles that did not concern immigration or asylum flows into the United Kingdom. The final sample was 119 articles, again drawn from the *Express* (24), the *Sun* (22), the *Daily Mail* (21), the *Telegraph* (16), the *Mirror* (13), *The Times* (13), and the *Guardian* (10). Some papers produced a larger quantity of articles, and this led to differences in the number of total articles from each paper on key stories relating to asylum and immigration during the period sampled. Of these 119 articles, 69 discussed asylum issues specifically, or asylum alongside economic migration, and most data trends were drawn from this category unless otherwise stated (*Sun* – 10, *Daily Mail* – 14, *Express* – 17, *The Times* – 8, *Telegraph* – 10, *Mirror* – 5, *Guardian* – 5). A further 36 articles either discussed 'immigrants', often without it being clear which type of migrant was being discussed, or referred to a story that concerned all categories of immigrants, including asylum seekers and refugees. Three articles focused on refugees, and eight specifically discussed economic migrants.

- *Daily Mail* (11 June 2011) 'Quaffing bubbly in a Bristol nightclub, Mugabe's torturer'
- *Daily Mail* (17 June 2011) 'Human right to sponge off UK'
- *Daily Mail* 1 (20 June 2011) 'Judges in scathing attack on the abuse of migrant appeals'
- *Daily Mail* 2 (20 June 2011) '*Daily Mail* comment: rights that make a mockery of justice'
- *Daily Mail* (21 June 2011) 'Cuts to legal aid for asylum cases'
- *Daily Mail* 1 (23 June 2011) 'UK fears migrant influx as EU bids to relax rules'
- *Daily Mail* 2 (23 June 2011) 'Voodoo terror of teen girls brought to UK as sex slaves'
- *Daily Mail* (29 June 2011) 'Secure Britain … what a joke'
- *Daily Mail* (30 June 2011) 'Cameron vowed to fix this: so why has he gone quiet?'
- *Sun* 1 (2 June 2011) 'Asylum amnesty outrage'
- *Sun* 2 (2 June 2011) 'Migrant luxury'
- *Sun* (4 June 2011) '£2bn legal raid: taxpayers' huge court cases bill'
- *Sun* 1 (15 June 2011) 'Big bill in age row'
- *Sun* 1 (23 June 2011) 'Letters: Emily, from Warrington'
- *Sun* 2 (23 June 2011) 'Out of border: EU plan to let illegals stay in Britain'
- *Sun* 3 (23 June 2011) 'Cam war on illegals'
- *Sun* 1 (25 June 2011) 'Eur-eka, PM!'
- *Sun* 2 (25 June 2011) 'PM fury at EU's £280m "palace"'
- *Sun* (29 June 2011) 'Ban on boot for foreign villains; Euro court says Britain must protect them'
- *Guardian* 1 (2 June 2011) '160,000 asylum seekers granted amnesty by the backdoor, say MPs: another 74,500 cases "cannot be traced" – report minister hails elimination of backlog from system'
- *Guardian* 2 (2 June 2011) 'Reply: letter: access to university and asylum seekers'
- *Guardian* (22 June 2011) 'Rape victim to be deported despite ongoing investigation'
- *Guardian* (23 June 2011) 'Cameron to challenge EU plan to amend asylum rule'

- *Guardian* (28 June 2011) 'Front: the nanny's story "I was treated like a slave"'
- *The Times* 1 (2 June 2011) 'Amnesty given to 160,000 asylum seekers; "you can stay" solution is used to clear Border Agency backlog'
- *The Times* 2 (2 June 2011) 'Asylum amnesty allows thousands to stay; in the news'
- *The Times* 1 (3 June 2011) 'The week'
- *The Times* 2 (3 June 2011) 'Letters: asylum: it's not a numbers game'
- *The Times* (6 June 2011) 'Letters: government delays and asylum seekers'
- *The Times* (17 June 2011) 'DNA test for bogus refugees scrapped as expensive flop'
- *The Times* 1 (29 June 2011) 'Islamist preacher barred from UK due to speak at commons'
- *The Times* 2 (29 June 2011) 'Human rights court blocks deportations'
- *Mirror* (1 June 2011) 'Pounds 100K sorry for HIV bite; Compo'
- *Mirror* (2 June 2011) '160,000 in asylum 'amnesty'; they're allowed to stay here'
- *Mirror* (3 June 2011) 'Pounds 1 million for immigration "chaos" boss; asylum'
- *Mirror* (16 June 2011) 'Bail denied to rape case Ethiopian; asylum'
- *Mirror* 1 (23 June 2011) 'Asylum rate "set to soar"; Europe'
- *Telegraph* (2 June 2011) 'Errors "allowed an asylum amnesty"'
- *Telegraph* 1 (3 June 2011) 'Britain's borders are still wide open to abuse by migrants'
- *Telegraph* 2 (3 June 2011) 'Boss at top of immigration 'shambles' was paid £1m'
- *Telegraph* (7 June 2011) 'May's pledge to halt North African migrants'
- *Telegraph* (15 June 2011) 'Sri Lankan refugees face deportation'
- *Telegraph* (17 June 2011) '3,200 stay annually under "family rights"'
- *Telegraph* 1 (23 June 2011) 'Fight to keep migrant deportations'
- *Telegraph* 2 (23 June 2011) 'Cameron fights plan to suspend law on migrant deportations'
- *Telegraph* (25 June 2011) 'Cameron blocks EU plan to soften deportation law'

- *Telegraph* (29 June 2011) 'Britain cannot deport Somali criminals, European Court rules'
- *Express* (1 June 2011) 'Fury at £1m-a-month "bribes" to send illegal migrants home'
- *Express* 1 (2 June 2011) 'Britain opens door to asylum seekers'
- *Express* 2 (2 June 2011) 'Sending out a dangerous signal to asylum seekers; leader'
- *Express* 3 (2 June 2011) 'New centre to remove immigrants'
- *Express* 1 (3 June 2011) 'A terrible blow to hopes of getting a grip on migration'
- *Express* 2 (3 June 2011) 'Crisis talks in fight to stem migrant hordes'
- *Express* 3 (3 June 2011) 'Amnesty to way to tackle immigration problem; letters'
- *Express* 1 (6 June 2011) 'End this silly amnesty for so many asylum seekers; letters'
- *Express* 2 (6 June 2011) 'Scandal of illegals freed onto streets to clear backlog'
- *Express* 3 (6 June 2011) 'Theresa May'
- *Express* 4 (6 June 2011) 'UK message to migrants: You are not wanted'
- *Express* 1 (13 June 2011) 'Just what does it mean to be British these days?'
- *Express* (17 June 2011) 'Migrants use human rights law to sponge off taxpayers'
- *Express* (21 June 2011) 'Cameron: Lib Dems have put breaks on migrant crackdown'
- *Express* 1 (24 June 2011) 'PM: We won't budge over Greece bail-out'
- *Express* 2 (24 June 2011) 'Cameron wins battle over Greece bail-out'
- *Express* (30 June 2011) 'We must regain right to kick out foreign criminals'.

Further articles were also analysed and drawn on to provide wider context, but most of our data was derived using the above list, as we focused on asylum. The additional articles included these on refugees:

- *Daily Mail* 1 (13 June 2011) 'Now a retreat on benefits'
- *Sun* 2 (15 June 2011) 'Letters'
- *Guardian* (20 June 2011) 'Reply: letter: World Refugee Day'.

The following either dealt with immigration more broadly or it was not clear in the article what category of immigrant was being discussed:

- *Daily Mail* 3 (3 June 2011) 'Pilloried'
- *Daily Mail* (9 June 2011) 'Jailed for murder, immigrant who should have been deported in 2002'
- *Daily Mail* 2 (13 June 2011) '100 offenders beat deportation'
- *Daily Mail* (18 June 2011) 'Australia to send *Silence of the Lambs* rapist back to UK'
- *Daily Mail* (25 June 2011) 'Cameron has finally woken up to the disaster that is immigration. But he's left it too late.'
- *Sun* 3 (2 June 2011) 'Migrants amnesty'
- *Sun* (6 June 2011) 'TXT US'
- *Sun* (7 June 2011) 'Get tough on law and border'.
- *Sun.* (9 June 2011) 'Nicked at wedding'
- *Sun* 1 (13 June 2011) '"Student" visa drop'
- *Sun* 2 (13 June 2011) 'Migrant crooks in new ruse'
- *Sun* 3 (13 June 2011) 'Foreign lags ruse on family'.
- *Sun* (21 June 2011) 'Plane slash'
- *Sun* (24 June 2011) 'Illegal on May train'
- *Guardian* (10 June 2011) 'Migrant plan will harm recovery, May warned: restricting workers could be "disruptive" to business. Wealthiest migrants to be exempt from rules.'
- *Guardian* (21 June 2011) 'We'd be harder on immigration without the Lib Dems, says PM'
- *The Times* 3 (2 June 2011) 'A new name but same old problems'
- *The Times* 3 (3 June 2011) 'Afghan bomber radicalised in British jail, say investigators'
- *The Times* (9 June 2011) 'Life for illegal immigrant who killed homeless man'
- *The Times* (20 June 2011) 'Fighting for business, street by street; Monday manifesto everybody takes their turn on the front line at Lebara, even the mobile network's boss'
- *The Times* (21 June 2011) 'Farmer put illegal workers' waste into burn; five warnings from Environment Agency defied'
- *Mirror* (13 June 2011) 'Untouchable; 102 foreign offenders UK can't deport because of their right to a family'

- *Mirror* (18 June 2011) 'Two "illegal" workers are arrested; employment'
- *Mirror* 1 (21 June 2011) 'Plane man slits neck'
- *Mirror* 2 (21 June 2011) 'Deportee cuts own throat on plane to Jamaica; terror on flight'
- *Mirror* (24 June 2011) 'Illegal immigrant found on Theresa May's train; he was on board as she checked border'
- *Telegraph* (20 June 2011) 'Migrants take 9 out of 10 jobs, says Field; "public wants tougher rules on welfare"'
- *Telegraph* 1 (21 June 2011) 'Illegal migrant slashes throat on Virgin jet; news bulletin'
- *Telegraph* 2 (21 June 2011) 'Plan to halve jail terms for guilty pleas scrapped'
- *Express* 4 (2 June 2011) 'Don't squander our money on illegal immigrants; letters'
- *Express* 2 (13 June 2011) 'War on bogus students to cut migrants'
- *Express* 3 (13 June 2011) 'Scandal of foreign crooks we can't kick out of Britain'
- *Express* (14 June 2011) '"Scandal" of tax cash to migrants'
- *Express* (20 June 2011) 'Nine out of ten jobs go to migrants because of lazy Britons'
- *Express* 3 (24 June 2011) '97,000 "hidden" migrants who work in Britain'
- *Express* 4 (24 June 2011) 'Streets and schools where English is a foreign language'

The following articles dealt with economic migration:

- *Daily Mail* (5 June 2011) 'Dave must show that his word is law … not Ken's'
- *Sun* (24 June 2011) 'A third of migrants "missing"'
- *Guardian* (18 June 2011) 'Australia to deport dungeon sex offender to UK'
- *Mirror* (10 June 2011) 'Immigration clamp down will damage UK recovery'
- *Mirror* (18 June 2011) 'Dungeon rape fiend is dumped on Britain'
- *Mirror* 2 (23 June 2011) 'Asylum con made pounds 250k; deported'
- *Telegraph* (13 June 2011) 'Cuts in foreign students scaled back'

- *Telegraph* (20 June 2011) '"These welfare reforms won't hit the spot." Coalition changes to the benefits system fly in the face of what voters would like to see'.

By 2011, numbers of asylum applications had been sustained at a level of 25,932 or below for a period of seven years (2005–2011) (Blinder, 2011), so for the 2011 coverage we re-examined the same eight themes as for 2006, to identify possible variations between the two periods:

- conflation of forced and economic migration
- numbers and exaggeration
- burden on welfare and job market
- criminality, threat, deportation and human rights
- the need for 'immigration control'
- the benefits of immigration
- problems facing asylum seekers
- global capitalism, imperialism and western responsibility.

Who Speaks

We considered the range of voices included in the 69 sampled articles that discussed asylum (or asylum alongside economic migration), and the positions they took on support, resources, and the right to remain in the United Kingdom for the migrants discussed. Statements and sources cited by the journalists in the articles were most commonly attributed to politicians; 74 statements across the 69 articles. Just two of these quotes positively supported the provisions with respect to the migrants discussed, while 30 were critical, such as the *Telegraph* reporting that the home secretary:

> Theresa May has pledged to stop tens of thousands of migrants who are fleeing the turmoil in North Africa from flooding Britain .... Mrs May said she was concerned about people from North African countries caught up in the Arab Spring unrest trying to settle in Britain.
>
> (*Telegraph*, 7 June 2011)

There were 146 reported statements in all, and just five of these were from asylum seekers/refugees themselves, 3.4 per cent of the total.

These were found twice in the *Guardian* and three times in the *Daily Mail*. NGOs or migrant organizations were cited five times in the sample, twice in the *Guardian* and three times in the *Telegraph*. Two of these statements specifically supported migrants' rights, including an example in *The Times* of a letter from Red Cross spokesperson George McNamara, who stated that 'concern about the number of asylum cases being approved cannot be a pretext for refusal, resulting in people being sent back to situations where they would be in danger' (*The Times* 2, 3 June 2011). We also identified 19 statements from judges and lawyers, of whom ten argued in support of those migrants they were discussing but it is important to note that these were often included within articles otherwise wholly critical of the judges' ruling. For example, one article describes: 'the sickening story of the man who told the Home Office he enjoyed torture and the judge who says it's his human right to stay here' (*Daily Mail,* 11 June 2011). Four judges' statements were critical, for example arguing the cases were 'without merit'. The anti-immigration think-tank Migration Watch was quoted ten times and was very critical on the issues of support, resources, or right to remain. For example, it argued that 'the key now is to be far more effective at removing those asylum seekers whose claims fail...' (*Daily Mail* 1, 3 June 2011). These references appeared commonly in the tabloids, particularly the *Express* (six times), but also three times in the *Mail* and once in the *Sun*. Of the total 146 statements recorded for quoted speakers, 51 made negative and critical statements, and 20 made statements that were supportive.

Conflation of Forced and Economic Migration

On TV News

The conflation of asylum issues within economic migration or 'illegal immigration' was less pronounced in TV coverage in 2011 than in 2006, though it still occurred. The phrase 'illegal immigrant' (or variations thereof, including 'illegals' or 'illegal population') appeared in 4/5 of the TV news broadcasts (not featuring at all in ITV *Lunchtime News*), but in the broadcasts that did use this term, it was used only once. In one example, *Channel 4 News* treated asylum seekers as a category of 'illegal immigrants', the correspondent stating that 'In the run-up to the election, the LibDem leader proposed an amnesty for all illegal immigrants, *not just* asylum seekers' (*Channel 4 News*, 2 June 2011 – original emphasis).

Overall, the broadcasters used the term 'asylum seekers' more appropriately in discussing the 'amnesty' story, and the term 'irregular migrants' was used by a presenter in one instance to refer to those who had come with an economic motive: 'During the election Tory immigration spokesman Damian Green accused the Liberal Democrats of proposing a dangerous amnesty for irregular migrants who had been in Britain for more than ten years (BBC1 *10 O'Clock News*, 2 June 2011).

Preceding this however, the same report began with strong opening words from Damian Green implying that an amnesty invited 'illegal immigration': 'If you have an amnesty you wave a flag around the world saying "Come to this country, stay illegally for long enough"'. A clear equivalence was drawn between the suggested 2010 amnesty for 'irregular migrants' (including economic migrants) and the 2011 'amnesty' which concerned only asylum seekers (BBC1 *10 O'Clock News*, 2 June 2011). Later in the programme on-screen figures relating to how the asylum backlog was dispatched were shown. These were followed by the word 'Immigration'. The story was then further established as an 'immigration' issue: the programme showed a clip of David Cameron from 2010 stating 'I'd like to see net migration come down to the level of the '80s and '90s where it would be more like tens of thousands.' These asylum decisions were thus positioned in relation to a concern with the numbers in and numbers out. This was further reinforced by the presenter, who introduced on-screen numbers for net migration, again with the title 'Immigration' on screen followed by '142,000'. The presenter said, 'When the coalition came to power net migration was put at 142,000.' The number then changed and a big red UP arrow appeared to emphasise the increase, as the presenter stated, 'The latest figures show it has risen to 242,000. Now, the causes are not actually in the government's control: emigration, people leaving Britain, is down, and immigration from other EU countries is up.' The closing words also reinforced this analysis: 'Politicians want to sound tough but when they are faced with the complexities of immigration they find it hard to get their rhetoric to match the reality' (BBC1 *10 O'Clock News*, 2 June 2011).

Where conflation did occur, this was often more subtle than in 2006. For example, on ITV *News at 10* two asylum seekers were interviewed. The first, a Sri Lankan refugee Fis Bellingim, was asked, 'When did you come to the UK and why did you come to this country?' He was not asked 'Why did you seek asylum?' and his reasons for fleeing were not described. Bellingim's answer came through an interpreter: 'There some other countries, they're not issuing, granting asylum, um, this country people say is granting asylum, that's why I came here.' This could prompt the question why other countries are not letting asylum seekers in, but inside the wider narrative of the programme, it prompted the question why the United Kingdom *was* doing so. Following a detailed exposition of numbers with images of crowds (as mentioned above), the programme moved on to the second interview. The voiceover said, 'Forfana, from Sierra Leone, who does not want to be identified, says there is a simple reason why people like him go underground.' Then Forfana, his face blurred, described how 'A lot of people are underground because they are scared to appear. Because they scared you they say if we hold you, you go to prison' (ITV *News at Ten,* 2 June 2011).

The programme did not discuss why Forfana or other asylum seekers might be so scared of becoming known to the authorities and being sent to a detention centre. This issue was raised in our interviews. We were told (by a refugee worker who is a Sri Lankan refugee) that refugees are sometimes driven underground by a fear that the asylum process is a 'lottery' and by not wishing to risk their claim being wrongly rejected and deportation, despite their having a genuine fear of persecution.

Forfana's account was followed by the image of a critical election advertisement on the side of a van, which read '"We don't know how many illegal immigrants there are but they're welcome to stay. And bring a mate." LibDem Manifesto 2010.' The correspondent's voiceover states that 'An amnesty for immigrants was an idea floated by the Liberal Democrats during last year's election campaign, an idea much criticised by David Cameron in TV debates.' This conflated the discussion of asylum issues which preceded it (the alleged 2011 'amnesty' only concerned asylum claims) with an amnesty proposed for 'immigrants' in general. We were then shown footage of a televised election debate from April 2010 in which Cameron said, 'The idea of the amnesty, it's been shown all over Europe that what that leads to is a big increase in false asylum claims', a statement which was left unquestioned.

The programme again equated the processing of long-term asylum cases in 2011 to what was proposed in 2010 for all immigrants. Its correspondent stated, 'But the committee of MPs who wrote today's report say an amnesty this certainly is' (ITV *News at Ten*, 2 June 2011). The word 'amnesty' thus was used to conflate the two issues, and the suggestion of so-called 'illegal immigrants' being allowed to stay was not seen as distinct from the clearing of the backlog by giving leave to stay to long-term asylum seekers who might by then have established connections to the United Kingdom. This was also implied by the words of Home Affairs Select Committee chair, Labour MP Keith Vaz: 'No minister wants to say that there is going to be an amnesty on immigration because he or she will be perceived to be soft on immigration. We're just stating the facts' (ITV *News at Ten*, 2 June 2011).

Another example, from BBC1 *Lunchtime News*, also conflated the categories of immigration and asylum in its use of language and the presentation of the story. Its headline, 'Soft on immigration – the government is accused of allowing so many asylum seekers into the country that it amounts to an amnesty', clearly positioned asylum decisions within the wider 'immigration' debate, yet the item was concerned with the asylum 'amnesty' story. After the presenter had introduced the Home Affairs Select Committee's main criticisms, the report began with footage of Morton Hall Removal Centre and a voiceover saying:

> For thousands of illegal immigrants these fences are the last thing they'll see before being forced to leave the UK. Rejecting their applications to stay can be a lengthy process. A report by the Home Affairs Committee says the UK Border Agency has failed to do it adequately.
>
> (BBC1 *Lunchtime News*, 2 June 2011)

In fact the report concerned asylum seekers, many of whom had not exhausted their appeals, not 'illegal immigrants'. As the report cut to show its on-screen computer-generated figures, the word 'immigration' appeared before the figures, and the notion of the story being an immigration issue was reinforced. Then later, in his closing remarks, the presenter stated that 'The government intend to reduce immigration from hundreds of thousands a year to tens of thousands, but today's report, and cuts to the Border Agency budget, cast doubt over its chances of success,' reaffirming that these were 'immigrants' that were being discussed, not refugees (BBC1 *Lunchtime News*, 2 June 2011).

While ITV *Lunchtime News* did not use the term 'illegal immigrant', clear suggestions that the asylum seekers might not be 'genuine' recurred throughout. For example, the studio presenter, interviewing Damian Green, said, 'You've denied all morning that this is an amnesty as Keith Vaz has suggested but you have eased the rules; basically this message being, "Keep your head down for six to eight years and you'll get away with it"' (ITV *Lunchtime News*, 2 June 2011). The presenter later called into question whether the individuals were actually 'asylum seekers', suggesting that this language could 'confuse' the public:

> One thing that may confuse or concern people is the language here – 'asylum seekers'. If you say someone is living in fear of their life in some country because of their religious beliefs or perhaps their sexual preference or what have you, that's asylum, they need to be looked after. Half a million people coming here saying 'I need asylum'?

Damian Green responded to this by clarifying that the 'half a million' was the backlog of cases that had built up in 2005. They did not arrive all at once; he said that 'The number of people who applied for asylum last year was 20,000, and we can cope with that.' That the asylum claims took so long to process did not mean they were any more likely to have been false, and it cannot be concluded from this that the 161,000 who were allowed to stay were not 'genuine'. The presenter then pointed to the effects on people who live in fear of their lives, so in this sense the real needs of some people were highlighted, which in the news coverage overall is comparatively rare, although the context was of people abusing the system: 'But it is a system, is it not, finally,

Minister, that allows some people to make a real mockery of those men and women who genuinely live in fear of their lives in certain countries?' (ITV *Lunchtime News*, 2 June 2011).

In the Press

Most articles covering asylum issues discussed these alongside economic migration issues, which meant that in the 2011 sample 56 of the 69 articles which discussed asylum issues had a very negative tone. Across all 69 articles in the 2011 sample where asylum seekers were discussed, the term 'illegal immigrant' (or variations such as 'illegals' or 'illegal population') appeared 48 times. Sixteen of these were found in the *Express* and eleven in the *Sun*, eight in the *Mail*, and seven in the *Telegraph*. In these papers there was little discernible change in how the terms were used in relation to asylum issues. However, the *Guardian* and *The Times* only used the term once, and it was not found in the *Mirror*. In an article the following month, the *Guardian* used the phrase 'undocumented immigrants' to describe Pulitzer Prize winner Antonio Vargas (*Guardian*, 27 July 2011), who recently revealed his status and also has commented publicly on the 'simplistic us-versus-them' immigration coverage (Vargas, 2011). The term is rarely used in the media. In a search across the whole year's coverage, in 2006 we found the phrase used in two articles, and in 2011 we found it in four articles, all in the *Guardian* or *The Times*. The term 'undocumented immigrant' is preferred by the United Nations, other international organisations and refugee groups as a less problematic and confusing alternative to 'illegal immigrant'.

Beyond the change in these few articles, the conflation of asylum issues under the banner of 'illegal immigrant' was widespread. For example, in the *Telegraph*, readers were told at the start that 'David Cameron is to insist that illegal immigrants are deported to the European country where they first arrived' (*Telegraph* 2, 23 June 2011). These 'illegal immigrants' were then described as people 'fleeing the troubles in North Africa and the Middle East' (*Telegraph* 2, 23 June 2011). The story concerned prime minister David Cameron's rejection of EU proposals to stop countries deporting asylum seekers to the European country to which they first arrived, a practice which placed a disproportionate burden on countries like Greece. The paper then quoted the UNHCR's assertion that the people face a 'humanitarian crisis' in Greece and to stay there violates their human rights.

This article clearly acknowledged that the migrants came from 'Arab Spring' countries and mentioned asylum rules, yet the people it discussed were referred to twice as 'illegal immigrants' and also frequently as 'immigrants', a term which obfuscates the point that many will be fleeing conflict (*Telegraph* 2, 23 June 2011). A statement that these were 'refugees' was actually made by Cecilia Malmstrom, the EU 'immigration chief' in the article, which stated that she 'has accused EU governments of allowing xenophobic sentiments in Europe to dictate immigration policy and failing to protect refugees from North Africa' (*Telegraph* 2, 23 June 2011). But the journalist then followed up the quoted statements by again using the language of 'immigrants' to discuss people including those just described as refugees: 'It is believed that up to 1,500 immigrants may have died trying to reach countries in southern Europe so far this year' (*Telegraph* 2, 23 June 2011).

In another example, the *Telegraph* stated that home secretary Theresa May intended to stop 'tens of thousands of migrants who are fleeing the turmoil in North Africa from flooding Britain'. It reported her concern that 'people caught up in the Arab Spring unrest' might try to settle in Britain (7 June 2011). Despite this 'unrest', the word 'asylum' was notably absent, and the piece instead referred to stopping 'illegal immigrants' (*Telegraph*, 7 June 2011).

In a third article the *Telegraph* commented that 'the law change would have allowed illegal immigrants to make their way across Europe to Britain before claiming asylum' (*Telegraph*, 25 June 2011). The *Sun* called this an 'EU plan to let illegals stay in Britain' (*Sun* 2, 23 June 2011). The *Express* likewise discussed 'illegal immigrants', although it pointed out that 'all have escaped turmoil in countries like Tunisia, Egypt and Libya' (*Express* 2, 3 June 2011).

A piece by Theresa May in the *Express* stated that 'we will not agree to so-called "burden-sharing" – Britain will not be accepting large numbers of African migrants' (*Express* 3, 6 June 2011). She again failed to acknowledge that many of those coming from Africa were asylum seekers, repeatedly calling them 'illegal immigrants' and 'migrants', which avoided any notion of responsibility for 'burden-sharing' to ease the strain on Greece (*Express* 3, 6 June 2011).

In contrast we can see alternative reporting on this same issue from outside our sample in the *Independent* from May, which referred to the people fleeing the Arab Spring as 'refugees', in both the headline, 'Arab Spring refugees not welcome here, says William Hague' and the body text, which stated that 'last week the Home Secretary, Theresa May, resisted calls from Italy, which has borne the brunt of *thousands of refugees* crossing the Mediterranean, for other EU countries to "share the burden" of accommodating the new arrivals' (23 May 2011 – our emphasis).

Once again, we found in our sample of 69 articles that the conflation of asylum seekers with 'migrants' in general was sometimes underpinned by the assumption that people entering outside the usual channels, or without documentation, must be 'illegal immigrants'. We found eleven pejorative references to 'illegal entry' (and similar terms such as 'sneaking in'), five of which were in the *Express*. The *Sun* article cited above referred to Cameron's bid to fight the EU changes to asylum seeker returns. These changes, the article claimed, would mean that 'immigrants who *sneak into* the UK from France could no longer be sent back to be dealt with by French authorities' (*Sun* 2, 23 June 2011 – our emphasis). The *Daily Mail* stated that the Border Agency's 'default setting is to rubber-stamp applications for asylum, *even where the claimant has sneaked into the country illegally*, or been involved in dreadful crimes' (*Daily Mail*, 30 June 2011 – our emphasis). As there is often no way asylum seekers can escape and travel by complying with ordinary border controls, the Refugee Convention of which the United Kingdom is a signatory states that they should not be penalized and treated differently because they have entered the country clandestinely (UNHCR, 1951).

The deportation of rejected asylum seekers was mentioned in 28 of 69 articles discussing asylum or asylum and economic migrants together (including seven in the *Mail*, five in the *Express* and five in the *Sun*). In a clear example from the *Daily Mail*, rejected asylum seekers were bracketed with 'illegal immigrants'. Sir Andrew Green of Migration Watch was first quoted as saying, 'The key now is to be far more effective in removing those asylum seekers whose claims fail at the end of a very long and expensive process' (*Daily Mail* 1, 3 June 2011).

This is followed by the journalist's statement equating these failed claims with 'illegal immigration': 'The most recent Home Office figures showed asylum applications were up 10% last quarter, but the number of illegal immigrants deported fell 5%' (*Daily Mail* 1, 3 June 2011).

An article discussing legal aid and deportation in the *Mail* stated that 'The Justice Secretary will cut funding for lawyers who repeatedly challenge decisions to kick out illegal immigrants, and reduce the £90 million spent on asylum and immigration cases each year'[2] (*Daily Mail*, 21 June 2011). But asylum seekers who rely on legal aid, and who may have their asylum claims rejected, are not necessarily economic migrants claiming asylum fraudulently. There are many reasons why a claim might be rejected in error or by accident. Yet the assumption that most people seeking asylum are frauds shapes much of the debate.

One *Express* article also cited Sir Andrew Green of Migration Watch, saying that 'two thirds of those people who claim to be asylum seekers are rejected. If you are serious about granting asylum to refugees you have to be equally serious about removing those who turn out to be bogus' (*Express* 1, 3 June 2011). It then stated that the policy of granting asylum to people who had been waiting a long time in order to clear a backlog 'not only offends natural justice but sends a powerful signal back to the countries producing the most asylum seekers that tells new waves of false claimants it is worth them coming to Britain to try their luck' (*Express* 1, 3 June 2011).

This issue was often framed as an issue of sovereignty in relation to Europe, as when the *Sun* argued that:

> Miracles will never cease. David Cameron has stood up to Brussels. The PM has won his fight to stop Britain being forced to contribute to the latest Greece rescue fund. He has seen off an attempt to stop Britain expelling bogus asylum seekers.
>
> (*Sun* 1, 25 June 2011)

The *Guardian* also discussed deportation in two more positive articles.

---

2 There was no response given from members of the legal profession in the article, only one quotation from a 'Ministry of Justice' spokesperson.

One pointed out that African asylum seekers could not be returned to Greece 'because of the state of its reception centres', and cited figures from Frontex (the EU border management agency) estimating that 1,200 of the 48,000 people who had fled to Europe had died at sea (*Guardian*, 23 June 2011).

Pressure for deportation, and the portrayal of asylum seekers as fraudulent 'illegals', was supported by language such as 'asylum cheats', 'frauds', 'bogus asylum seekers' and 'scamming', which occurred 14 times in the articles discussing asylum. *The Times*, for instance, in one article about DNA testing to prove nationality, used the phrase 'bogus refugees' in the headline. It also talked of 'Kenyans trying to pass themselves off as war refugees from Somalia' (*The Times*, 17 June 2011). One *Express* article talked of the 'amnesty' allowing 'bogus refugees' to claim benefits (*Express* 1, 13 June 2011). In addition to this, the 'abuse' or 'exploitation' of the British asylum/legal system or borders was mentioned 19 times in 2011 coverage of asylum seekers. Most of these references (twelve) were found in the *Mail*, representing an increase in 2011 over the five references in this category in the 2006 sample. An example is the headline in the *Telegraph*, 'Britain's borders are still wide open to abuse by migrants' (*Telegraph* 1, 3 June 2011). This reflects a common assumption in coverage of the asylum system, that most asylum seekers are fraudulent and the system exists to expose their 'bogus claims', rather than to assess the needs of people who are refugees.

Threatening Numbers

On TV News

Emphasis on numbers was the strongest theme in the TV sample. Some discussion of numbers was to be expected, as all news reports focused on the criticism made by the Home Affairs Select Committee of the way in which the 2006 backlog of asylum seekers had been processed. However, the emphasis was on 'numbers coming in' as undesirable, as opposed to the human impact of keeping large numbers of people in a state of uncertainty and fear of deportation for a period of years, which could equally have been discussed.

Often in the newsreader's opening headline or introductory words, vague and indeterminate language was used to communicate the sense of large threatening numbers. On ITV *News at Ten* for example the headline was 'An amnesty in all but name: how thousands of asylum seekers remain in Britain, unchallenged and unchecked' (2 June 2011). This was accompanied by the image of people congregating in a waiting area. On the BBC1 *10 O'Clock News* the headline was 'How hundreds of thousands of asylum seekers have been allowed to stay in the UK. MPs say it amounts to an amnesty.' The sense of size was reinforced once the main body of news began, since the presenter said that:

> So many asylum seekers have been allowed to remain in the UK that it amounts to an *amnesty*, according to a group of MPs. The huge backlog of almost half a million cases identified five years ago has been drastically cut but the Home Affairs Committee isn't happy with the way that's been achieved.
>
> (BBC1 *10 O'Clock News*, 2 June 2011)

Language such as 'so many ... that' and 'huge backlog', and vague, rounded-up numbers such as 'almost half a million' suggested uncontrolled immigration. Later in the report the correspondent said that 'Mr Green has admitted that tens of thousands of asylum seekers whose cases have never been investigated are being allowed to stay in Britain, with *far fewer* being removed' (BBC1 *10 O'Clock News*, 2 June 2011 – programme's emphasis).

All the TV news broadcasts used computer-generated lists on screen to give a breakdown of the numbers processed in different ways. This was to show how the backlog was dispatched. In two of the five TV programmes sampled, unsourced data was found (ITV *Lunchtime News*, 2 June 2011 and BBC1 *10 O'Clock News*, 2 June 2011), but other broadcasts showed the source on screen. The onscreen figures were superimposed over graphics and images, and in all cases were simultaneously detailed by a correspondent's voiceover. Often the images served to reinforce a sense of large numbers. One example displayed numbers over a graphic of anonymous rows of computer-generated people, resembling an army. Sections of this graphic were lit up to show the proportion 'removed' or 'disappeared' (*Channel 4 News*, 2 June 2011). In ITV *News at Ten*, the figures were bookended by images of crowds. An UK passport opened to show a crowd of people with the text '450,000 unresolved cases'. This changed to someone checking a passport and '403,000 cleared', then to Border Agency officers in uniform and '36,000 claims rejected'. Next came a 'leave to remain stamp' and '161,000 granted leave to remain', before the screen returned to the picture of crowds and '74,000 not traced' (2 June 2011). The voiceovers often emphasised the numbers involved, reinforcing rather than questioning the criticisms made by the report. For example, in an ITV *News at Ten* report the correspondent said:

> The UK Border Agency had 450,000 unresolved cases to process by this summer; so far 403,000 *have* been cleared. Of those cleared 36,000, less than 9 per cent, were rejected and removed from the UK. 161,000 were allowed to stay because they had already been living here for between six and eight years, and 74,000 applicants could *not* be traced, one in six of the cases. The Agency has no idea who among them is in the country and who has left.
>
> (ITV *News at Ten*, 2 June 2011 – original emphasis)

The figure of 36,000 was restated as 'less than 9 per cent' to stress what a small proportion had been 'rejected and removed', and this was contrasted with the '74,000 applicants' who 'could *not* be traced'. Both these points were then emphasised and restated further as 'one in six of the cases' and 'the Agency has no idea who among them is in the country and who has left' (ITV *News at Ten*, 2 June 2011).

In each news broadcast these numbers were frequently repeated and restated, underscoring the sense of the threat that they were assumed to pose. Sometimes they were represented by images. For example the BBC1 *10 O'Clock News* showed an aerial view of Liverpool with the voiceover 'This illustrates the government's problem: a backlog of asylum cases equivalent to the population of Liverpool has been allowed to build up since the 1990s' (BBC1 *10 O'Clock News*, 2 June 2011).

In the Press

The press sample was largely characterised by the use of superlatives, and unsourced statistics were found in 24 of the sampled articles on asylum issues or asylum and economic migration, with most in the *Express* (ten). We found 25 instances of pejorative language used to evoke 'natural disaster' and exaggerated numbers in the articles that discussed asylum seekers, for instance 'an iceberg', 'swamped', 'soaring', 'waves', 'masses' and 'flooding in'. A large proportion of these, 15, were in the *Express*, and five were in the *Telegraph*. This language was particularly common among the papers in discussing the implications of EU plans to stop asylum seekers being sent back to 'first entry' countries like Greece, and Cameron's efforts to retain this right. One article described how EU laws might be 'relaxed to deal with a wave of immigrants' coming from 'Arab Spring' countries. Elsewhere in the article the phrase 'a flood of immigrants' was used (*Telegraph* 2, 23 June 2011).

An *Express* article referred to 'waves of false claimants … coming to Britain to try their luck' and 'hordes of desperate young men' creating social problems (*Express* 1, 3 June 2011). The *Express* also described how the United Kingdom was to 'block a mass influx of migrants flooding across the channel from France' (21 June 2011). Calais was still a focus, and there were multiple references particularly in the *Express* to people crossing the channel and 'The Jungle', a new camp which had formed, this time illegally, taking the place of Sangatte (*Express* 2, 3 June 2011).

In the *Sun*, one article discussed what it called 'a European bid to allow thousands of illegal immigrants to stay in Britain' (*Sun* 2, 23 June 2011). The article gave prominence to Migration Watch's research, saying that 'An immigration think-tank has revealed even the ban on sending asylum seekers back to Greece could see floodgates of new arrivals to the UK' (*Sun* 2, 23 June 2011). Sir Andrew Green of Migration Watch was then quoted in the closing words of the article: 'It will not be long before asylum seekers flock to Greece secure in the knowledge that if they can get to Britain, we will have to deal with their cases' (*Sun* 2, 23 June 2011).

Language was also used to justify a need for stronger border controls and attack the 'amnesty' policy of allowing many of the backlog of asylum cases to stay because of their family ties and length of time in the country. The *Express* said that 450,000 asylum seekers' case files 'were found abandoned in boxes at the Home Office five years ago' (21 June 2011). The *Daily Mail* made a comparison of scale in one article, with the phrase 'a city of illegals the size of Brighton is allowed to stay', using Migration Watch figures and taking as its starting point 'the 1990's' (*Daily Mail* 1, 3 June 2011).

Another *Daily Mail* article quoted a remark first attributed to the Judges Council, that 85 per cent of asylum cases are without 'merit'. In this article, a 'senior immigration judge', Sir Anthony May, discussed the asylum seekers he saw before tribunals. They were, he claimed, often on their third or fourth appeal. 'Let us say that 85% of them, *that is a figure I rather pluck out of the air* but it is of that order, are of no merit' (*Daily Mail* 1, 20 June 2011 – our emphasis). The *Daily Mail* used this figure again in another article without Sir Anthony's qualification: 'Shockingly, the judges estimate that 85 per cent of judicial reviews brought by asylum seekers, in some instances their third or fourth appeal, have no merit at all' (*Daily Mail* 2, 20 June 2011). This contrasts sharply with a statement from the Refugee Council that 'The proportion of appeals allowed has been in the range 25–30% in recent years, so a significant number of initial decisions are found to be wrong by the tribunal' (2013).

It is not our intention here to suggest that every claim for asylum is genuine in the sense that the claimant has a legitimate right to refugee status. But the media obsessions with numbers, threats posed and alleged fraud sit oddly with the facts of the dramatic decline of asylum applications between 2002 and 2011 and the criticisms of the UNHCR for the high number of refusals in the UK to grant refuge. This is not just an issue of inaccurate or partial media coverage. It amounts to the systematic stigmatization of people who are vulnerable, and as we will show in our interviews with refugees and those who work with them, to a real increase in social harm.

A Burden on Welfare and the Job Market

On TV News

The theme of the burden of asylum seekers was not prominent in the TV coverage in our sample, which looked at the asylum 'amnesty' story. One suggestion of cost was found in BBC1 *10 O'Clock News*, where the presenter said regarding suggestions of an 'amnesty' for asylum seekers 'Fighting for extradition through the courts would have been hugely costly and probably fruitless so a more practical solution was to let them stay and put resources into protecting our borders now' (BBC1 *10 O'Clock News*, 2 June 2011).

In one case, on the ITV *Lunchtime News*, an asylum seeker 'Whaid' was given an opportunity to assert that he would not be a burden to the country: 'I will be happy I have paper to go to work.... Just, I will be happy. I don't want nothing from this country; I want only paper – I will – I go to work. I don't want benefit, I don't want nothing' (ITV *Lunchtime News*, 2 June 2011).

In the Press

In the press, however, the idea that asylum seekers are a burden to the taxpayer was much stronger. It was often included as a minor, supporting theme, of 26 asylum (or asylum with economic migration) articles from 2011. The largest number of individual phrases referencing 'burden' were found in the *Mail* (nine out of 23) followed by the *Sun* (four) and the *Express* (seven). One example from the *Express* declared that 'we are now forced to support millions of people who have absolutely no connection to Britain, such as [the] 12-strong Ethiopian family recently given a huge house in East London at a cost to the taxpayer of more than GBP75,000 a year' (*Express* 1, 13 June 2011).

Immigration in general was described as 'dragging down wages and imposing a crippling burden on our infrastructure' (*Express* 1, 13 June 2011). The 'burden' was mentioned just once each in the *Guardian* and the *Mirror*.

We found 19 incidences of language such as 'pay-out', 'hand-out', 'scrounger', 'workshy' and 'benefit tourist' in those articles looking at asylum in 2011, of which nine were in the *Daily Mail*, and eight in the *Express*. Another article in the *Express* claimed that 'failed asylum seekers and illegal immigrants are being "bribed" to go home with more than £1 million of taxpayers' cash'. These claims were backed up with Gerard Batten of UKIP, who commented, 'These people must think they've hit the jackpot' (*Express*, 1 June 2011).

The debate mentioned above over the changes to EU policy for asylum seekers was described in the *Daily Mail* as 'opening the door to thousands of immigrants heading for Britain to claim more generous benefits than they could get elsewhere', clearly establishing money as the driving force (*Daily Mail* 1, 23 June 2011). This trend in asylum coverage occurred at a time of financial hardship, and during a month when wider press coverage of general 'immigration' included a statement from Labour MP Frank Field (who was given the role of 'poverty tsar' by Cameron's Coalition in 2010), covered in both the *Express* (20 June 2011) and the *Telegraph*, that 87 per cent of new jobs 'have gone to immigrants' and calling for 'tougher rules on welfare' (*Telegraph*, 20 June 2011).

We found one article in the *Mail* that described 'a former asylum seeker', not identified as a refugee, who 'along with his wife and their seven children, was given a £2.1 million luxury townhouse at public expense' (*Daily Mail* 1, 13 June 2011).

Much was made of the perceived extravagance of the new detention centre, Morton Hall. The *Daily Mail* claimed that 'Officials refused to disclose how much Morton Hall cost to refurbish or operate. An official report into a smaller detention centre, which held just 124 people, found it cost £1.6 million every year' (*Daily Mail* 1, 2 June 2011). The article said that 'Critics said taxpayers will be angry that their money has been spent on conditions some hard-working families struggle to afford for themselves' (*Daily Mail* 1, 2 June 2011). Another article in the *Sun* ran with the headline 'Migrant luxury' (*Sun* 2, 2 June 2011). Similarly, in the Scottish *Sun* from 11 November 2011 (outside our sample), an article headlined '£80m benefits spree for asylum seekers' declared that Glasgow's asylum seekers receive 'a whopping £80 MILLION in benefits as they wait to find out if they can stay. More than 9,500 immigrants have shared the colossal sum for housing, clothes, food and living costs in Glasgow since 2004 as their papers were processed.'

This 'benefits spree' headline and other coverage enphasising the 'burden' of asylum on taxpayers should be considered in the context of rules governing provisions for asylum seekers. They are denied the right to work and are given vouchers worth less than the level of benefits, which is considered the minimum amount people can live on in the United Kingdom.

Another issue raised in some asylum stories was the reduction in entitlement to legal aid for those fighting deportation. This was mentioned four times in the sample of 69, all in articles supporting the reduction. The *Sun*, in an article entitled '£2bn legal raid; taxpayers huge court cases bill', stated that 'illegal immigrants trying to stay here can all be funded by legal aid' (*Sun*, 4 June 2011). Often the issue of the asylum seekers' legal expenses being paid was raised in articles on criminal cases, as in another *Mail* article, which mentioned that 'both were granted thousands in legal aid' (*Daily Mail*, 29 June 2011). A few months later in December 2011, an article from outside our sample, in the Scottish *Daily Mail,* falsely claimed Scotland was spending £5 million on the 'last ditch legal bids' or 'judicial reviews' of people claiming asylum. The correct figure was £0.6 million, and included 'judicial reviews for both asylum seekers and migrants'. The paper was subsequently forced to issue a correction (Scottish Refugee Council, 1 March 2012).

Outrage over the alleged burden to the taxpayer was strongest in relation to criminal cases in our sample. One *Daily Mail* headline claimed there was a 'Human right to sponge off UK' (17 June 2011). Likewise, the *Mail* said 'we are powerless to deport foreign criminals who have shamelessly abused this country's hospitality' on the basis of their human rights (*Daily Mail*, 30 June 2011). Another *Express* 'asylum' article backed up the general point with the blunt headline 'UK message to migrants: you are not wanted' (*Express* 4, 6 June 2011).

Criminality, Threat, Deportation and Human Rights

On TV News

A sense of 'threat' and connotations of criminality characterised the style of coverage of the asylum 'amnesty' story. This was constructed largely through the use of 'security' images demonstrating the control of a threat in all the broadcasts. For example in BBC1 *10 O'Clock News*, there were repeated images of immigration officials in uniform, prison-like images of fences, and images of a guard walking down a hallway with keys dangling by his side. This image was also used in BBC1 *Lunchtime News*. The theme of threat was also carried through reported statements in BBC1 *10 O'Clock News*, in the same example we refer to above, where the presenter stated that: 'Tory immigration spokesman Damian Green accused the Liberal Democrats of proposing a *dangerous* amnesty for irregular migrants who had been in Britain for more than ten years' (BBC1 *10 O'Clock News*, 2 June 2011 – our emphasis).

On *Channel 4 News* there were similar detention centre images, including asylum seekers being frisked by officials. Later in the report (as noted above) the presenter claimed that the amnesty was 'for all illegal immigrants, not just asylum seekers' (*Channel 4 News*, 2 June 2011), a statement that implies asylum seekers have done something illegal. Nick Clegg was then shown giving a speech from 2010: 'Please do not live in denial about what is going on. Don't live in denial about the fact that because of the chaos in the system we've got lots of people here who are working for criminal gangs rather than for Britain' (*Channel 4 News*, 2 June 2011).

We mentioned above the ITV *News at Ten* headline 'An amnesty in all but name: how thousands of asylum seekers remain in Britain, unchallenged and unchecked' (2 June 2011). This was accompanied by an image of people in a waiting area, including a mixed, though largely male, group of asylum seekers. Although the accompanying image was not threatening, the language describing them as 'unchallenged and unchecked' implied that a threat had been ignored. This programme and others also repeatedly represented asylum seekers as large crowds, and put a stress on the numbers.

In the Press

The potential threat was a strong press theme in the 2011 asylum sample. Crimes or other damage caused by asylum seekers were discussed in 14 articles (including four in the *Express* and five in the *Mail*), building the sense of 'public threat'. Roy Greenslade has pointed to a long history of the *Daily Mail* in particular associating asylum seekers with criminality (2005: 22). In the *Mirror* there were two examples of reporting of this kind. One article concerned an HIV-positive asylum seeker who had bitten her custody officer on the face. The officer described the experience as 'a living nightmare' (1 June 2011). Another concerned an asylum seeker from Ethiopia charged with rape, described by police in the article as a 'sexual predator' (*Mirror*, 16 June 2011). There was also one article in the *Mail* concerned with an incident of people trafficking, which focused on 'voodoo terror' and 'African black magic', and went into detail about the 'terrifying ceremony' and beliefs brought by 'migrant workers from the region', including the abuse of girls who had been trafficked and compelled to claim asylum (*Daily Mail* 2, 23 June 2011).

The *Express* also echoed a warning from Cameron that 'mass immigration had wrecked the social fabric and wiped out any sense of community in many areas' (21 June 2011). One *Express* article described immigration as 'a grotesque form of assisted national suicide', and highlighted its consequences as 'the spread of sharia law or the prevalence of violent gangs in our inner cities or the rise of Islamic extremism' (*Express* 1, 13 June 2011). It asserted that 'In the East London borough of Tower Hamlets, where there is a large Muslim population, gangs of zealots now roam the streets posing as self-appointed moral police, demanding that women wear the veil and that gay pubs be closed' (*Express* 1, 13 June 2011).

Coverage in the *Express* gave an overall sense of 'savagery'. It stressed the danger posed to the safety of British women by Asian and African 'men coming to Britain [who] often bring with them ... antediluvian attitudes' (*Express* 1, 3 June 2011). The article claimed that:

> This has had a massive impact on quality of life in many areas. New ghettos have sprung up. Large chunks of social housing have been diverted from Britons to foreigners. There has been extra pressure on the NHS as many of these incomers have arrived with conditions such as HIV.
>
> (*Express* 1, 3 June 2011)

The perceived threats brought by these groups from Asia and Africa, including 'conditions such as HIV' and a 'lack of respect for women's rights' led to an implication that 'life for British women is made less free and less safe as a result' (*Express* 1, 3 June 2011). The *Express* article argued that the Coalition lacked the 'willpower to protect communities from unwanted arrivals' (*Express* 1, 3 June 2011). The same *Express* article criticised all the mainstream parties: 'none of the main parties is in tune with public opinion on immigration and ulti-mately all appear willing to grant *hordes of desperate young men from poor countries* the de facto right to evade our laws' (*Express* 1, 3 June 2011 – our emphasis).

The implied 'threat' was found elsewhere too. For example, another

Express article claimed that an UKBA whistleblower had reported that 'illegal immigrants in detention centres are graded according to how dangerous they are perceived to be to the public' (*Express* 2, 6 June 2011). He went on to relate how 'In detention centres we have something called a "harm matrix". All detainees get graded A, B or C. When we're full up, we let out some Bs and Cs' (*Express* 2, 6 June 2011).

The theme of 'threat' was further developed through the debate over deportation of criminals or terrorists, subjects mentioned in 16 articles relating to asylum seekers (or asylum alongside economic migration) during 2011 (including six times in the *Mail* and four in the *Express*). The pejorative terms 'foreign prisoners' and 'foreign criminals' were noted 22 times in these articles relating to asylum seekers (or asylum alongside economic migration) during 2011. In one example, an article headlined 'Secure Britain ... what a joke' in the *Daily Mail*, a sense of threat was implied through the revelation that a 'Vile militant extremist strolls through Heathrow immigration'. The article went on to describe the person as 'an anti-semitic preacher of hate', before naming him as Raed Salah, a critic of Israel scheduled to speak at Westminster (*Daily Mail*, 29 June 2011). This unrelated event was confusingly laced in at the beginning of an article that primarily discussed refugees and asylum seekers convicted of serious offences who were appealing against deportation using the Human Rights Act.

Some articles contained direct attacks on the Human Rights Act or European Court of Human Rights, including eight from the *Mail*, seven in the *Sun* and eight in the *Express*. The *Mail* article mentioned above focused on the case of two Somalis granted the right to remain under Article 3 of the European Convention on Human Rights, which acts as a safeguard against inhumane treatment and torture. Judges had ruled they could not be sent back as they would face 'inhuman or degrading treatment', and awarded them court expenses. The article said they 'will be free to walk the streets', and stressed the implications for 214 other cases (*Daily Mail*, 29 June 2011). UKIP's Gerard Batten was quoted, saying that 'if foreign nationals prey on people here they should be sent home' (*Daily Mail*, 29 June 2011). The *Daily Mail* referred to the Act as a 'criminals' charter' twice in the article.

A *Sun* article opened with the statement 'Britain was yesterday banned from deporting hundreds of foreign killers, paedos and rapists by European judges' (29 June 2011). The story concerned the two Somali asylum seekers, who were described as 'thugs'. The article described 'hundreds of other foreign lags who claim they might face ill-treatment' (29 June 2011). The *Express* echoed this argument, presenting the situation as a systemic government weakness: 'The Government is so enfeebled that it cannot even deport even the most undesirable foreigners. It has been reported that more than 100 serious foreign criminals last year exploited human rights laws to escape deportation' (*Express* 1, 13 June 2011).

Another *Express* article argued that 'we are simply a vassal of unelected foreign judges, who determine some of the most basic areas of British law, whose decision is final and who care not a jot for the views of the British people' (*Express*, 30 June 2011) The paper claimed that the Somalis 'will now be free to walk the streets and carry on their life of crime' (*Express*, 30 June 2011). It claimed that the implications were 'horrifying in their scope', with criminals being 'protected at the expense of the public' (*Express*, 30 June 2011):

> Anyone – a serial killer, a paedophile, a drug baron or any other dangerous criminal – has the right to remain in the UK, free of any possible threat of deportation if their country of origin is in any way held to be unsafe. All because we are signatories of the European Convention on Human Rights.
>
> (*Express*, 30 June 2011)

The final claim made was that 'Some bleating liberals may protest but if Mr Cameron announced that Britain would no longer honour the European Convention, he would be the most popular Prime Minister in a generation' (*Express*, 30 June 2011).

The criminality argument was used in newspaper coverage to justify attacks on the UK Human Rights Act and arguments for 'immigration control'. In one *Express* article, a lorry driver making crossings to Calais was quoted as saying 'the Government has given these mafia gangs who control the trade a green ticket, they're going to be straight on the phone saying: Hey England is giving an amnesty' (*Express* 2, 3 June 2011). The stories about 'foreign criminals' coincide with the discussion elsewhere in the press of 'harm inflicted' by migrants, to create a strong theme of criminality and threat.

Need for 'Immigration Control'

On TV News

A need for 'immigration control' was a strong theme in TV coverage from 2011, epitomised by the headline on the BBC1 *Lunchtime News*, 'Soft on immigration – the government is accused of allowing so many asylum seekers into the country that it amounts to an amnesty'. After the presenter discussed the numbers, Keith Vaz stated that '161,000 people have been given the right to stay, so in effect it has been a silent amnesty. One in six cases being lost, it is clear that this agency isn't in control of the numbers who come in and out of this country' (BBC1 *Lunchtime News*, 2 June 2011).

An immigration officer was shown walking down a corridor, a familiar image, with keys swinging by his side, as the final voiceover said, 'The government intend to reduce immigration from hundreds of thousands a year to tens of thousands, but today's report, and cuts to the Border Agency budget, cast doubt over its chances of success' (BBC1 *Lunchtime News*, 2 June 2011).

The assertion that there had been an asylum 'amnesty' was taken as evidence of a weak immigration system. Words such as 'quietly' and Keith Vaz's phrase 'silent amnesty' (*Channel 4 News*, 2 June 2011) were frequently used to describe the government's actions and attack its own evasion of the phrase 'amnesty'. In ITV *News at Ten*, Keith Vaz said that 'no minister wants to say that there is going to be an amnesty on immigration because he or she will be perceived to be soft on immigration. We're just stating the facts' (2 June 2011).

Often the coverage of this theme stressed that the government's intentions were far from the reality, perceived as a lack of control. This was evident in the headline on ITV *News at Ten*, that 'thousands of asylum seekers remain in Britain, unchallenged and unchecked' (2 June 2011, quoted above). *Channel 4 News* included a series of comments made by Nick Clegg during a 2010 election debate, including that 'chaos in the system' justifies an amnesty for 'illegal immigrants'. The presenter closed the piece by saying:

Here at the Home Office the word is that the UK Border Agency is now fit for purpose, but is it? The government will in weeks publish figures showing a new backlog, many thousands of asylum cases still waiting to be processed. It's pretty clear ministers won't be able to blame their predecessors for much longer.

(*Channel 4 News*, 2 June 2011)

Some programmes raised the point that the rules had changed to allow people to stay if they had been waiting for six to eight years, without always stating that this was a policy brought in some time before, under the previous administration. *Channel 4 News* acknowledged this (2 June 2011), but it was omitted on ITV *News at Ten* (2 June 2011). The latter said that an asylum seeker 'had waited eight years. Previously applicants were required to live here for 12 years before being considered for permission' (2 June 2011), without clarifying when this ruling had changed. A presenter on BBC1 *10 O'Clock News* stated in a quote we also referred to above:

During the election Tory immigration spokesman Damian Green accused the Liberal Democrats of proposing a dangerous amnesty for irregular migrants who had been in Britain for more than ten years. Now he finds himself accused of sanctioning a silent amnesty for asylum seekers who have been here for more than six years.

(BBC1 *10 O'Clock News*, 2 June 2011)

Often the presenters seemed not to know when the policy had changed. The ITV *Lunchtime News* (2 June 2011) presenter said that '*New guidelines* say that if claimants have already lived here for six to eight years they can stay. Previously that was ten to twelve years' (our emphasis). Later in the programme (again, also see above) when the presenter was interviewing Damian Green, he said, 'You've denied all morning that this is an *amnesty* as Keith Vaz has suggested, but you *have* eased the rules, basically this message being, "keep your head down for six to eight years and you'll get away with it"' (2 June 2011 – original emphasis). Green corrected him: 'No, I haven't eased any rules at all ... that very specific relaxation of the rules happened in 2009, a year *before* the General Election' (again, original emphasis). In the BBC1 *10 O'Clock News* the same perceived disparity between government intentions and the reality was highlighted by the presenters. As mentioned above, this section involved an image of an immigration official with keys in a detention centre, and a voiceover:

> Opening a new detention centre the immigration minister wants to demonstrate the government's toughness. But, faced with a huge backlog, Mr Green has admitted that tens of thousands of asylum seekers whose cases have never been investigated have are being allowed to stay in Britain with *far fewer* being removed.
>
> (BBC1 *10 O'Clock News*, 2 June 2011 – original emphasis)

This time too Green promptly contradicted the claim, saying that '40 per cent of them have been granted leave to remain, which has been a figure that's ... been consistent, actually, since about 2005' (BBC1 *10 O'Clock News*, 2 June 2011). But we were then shown the aerial image of Liverpool (as noted above) and told 'a backlog of asylum cases, equivalent to the population of Liverpool has been allowed to build up since the 1990s'.

In the Press

The *Daily Mail* opened one story from our sample by asking 'Is Britain in control of its borders? After the events of recent days, the answer can only be a resounding "No"' (*Daily Mail*, 30 June 2011). It talked about 'immigration chaos', and twice referred to the Home Office as in a 'shambles'. In this and other articles during the period, the 'amnesty' ignited debate in the press over immigration control and the right to 'family life' under the Human Rights Act, which had enabled some asylum seekers to stay in the country. The article criticised Cameron's failure to pursue a British Bill of Rights. Previously, as a spokesperson for the opposition, he had been 'one of the most articulate voices about how the egregious Human Rights Act and the European Court of Human Rights had driven a coach and horses through our ability to police our own borders' (*Daily Mail*, 30 June 2011).

Now, however: 'the Government machine is engineered to continue with Labour's "open door" immigration policies' (*Daily Mail*, 30 June 2011). Attacking Raed Saleh's (aforementioned) visit, alongside its discussion of the 'amnesty' and the Somali case, this article criticised the Border Agency's failure to serve exclusion papers: 'it would be laughable if it were not so dangerous. After all, if a preacher on a "no-fly" watch list can do it, why not a banned terrorist?' This under-pinned the 'danger' posed by the assumed 'weakness' of Britain's border controls. The article went on to criticize strike action by Border Agency personnel: 'Yet how do our border guards respond? In their thousands, they are to join today's strike over public sector pensions, potentially leaving our borders even more exposed.' Its conclusion was that 'David Cameron could support his steely Home Secretary by finally doing something about the rampant abuse of the Human Rights Act. Britain's "secure borders" have been a bad joke for quite long enough.'

Similar attacks on the Act were found in the *Express*. One headline claimed 'Migrants use human rights law to sponge off taxpayers' (17 June 2011). It argued that 'most foreign criminals, failed asylum seekers and benefit tourists' used Article 8, the right to family life, 'to block Government attempts to deport them'. Another statement in this article was that 'the Home Office also revealed that Article 3 of the Human Rights Act – the right to protection from ill-treatment – was also used last year to prevent the removal of 56 foreign criminals and 16 asylum seekers'. All this meant, the article claimed, that 'Human Rights Law is threatening Britain's immigra-tion policy' and 'demolishing every aspect of the Government's tough stance on immigration'.

The need for 'immigration control' was a theme in 22 of 69 articles discussing asylum seekers (or asylum alongside economic migrants) in 2011, of which eight appeared in the *Express* and five in the *Mail*. The Home Affairs Select Committee called the approval of the 2011 asylum claims an 'amnesty', a phrase which was used in the press pejoratively to imply asylum had not been deserved and as evidence of Britain's 'open door policy'. Discussion of an 'asylum amnesty' occurred in 24 of the 69 articles (including nine times in the *Express*, and four times in both *The Times* and the *Mail*) but only once in the *Sun* and the *Guardian*. The word 'amnesty' was used 79 times in the 69 articles discussing asylum: 29 in the *Express*, 16 in the *Mail*, nine in the *Guardian* and eight times each in *The Times* and the *Telegraph*. One *Times* article was headed 'Asylum seeker amnesty allows thousands to stay' (*The Times* 2, 2 June 2011).

Often the emphasis in these articles was on the implied 'ease' of getting an asylum claim approved, as in the *Express*: 'Ministers seem to have decided it will do for them simply to appear to be getting a grip while in fact seeking shortcuts – in this case notionally clearing a backlog by nodding hundreds of thousands of people through' (*Express* 1, 3 June 2011).

Keith Vaz criticised the Borders Agency as being 'not fit for purpose' (a phrase originally used by John Reid in 2006), and this phrase was used to describe the asylum system or Borders Agency 19 times in the 2011 sample. Five of these mentions were in the *Express* and four in the *Telegraph*. Reference to 'wide-open Britain', the United Kingdom as a 'soft touch' or as having an 'open door policy', was a stronger theme in the 69 articles discussing asylum or asylum and economic migration in 2011 than in 2005. It occurred 14 times, of which eight were in the *Express*. For example, a leader in the *Express* responded to the 'amnesty' debate by arguing that 'Word that we are a soft touch got back to the countries that send us most asylum seekers long ago and so more arrive – most of them, in practice, economic migrants and so-called "benefit tourists"' (*Express* 2, 2 June 2011).

References to 'chaos' and similar terms (such as 'shambles', 'mockery' and 'fiasco) appeared 29 times in the 69 articles that discussed asylum issues (or asylum alongside economic migration) in 2011, including 13 in the *Mail* and eight in the *Express*. One such headline in the *Express* told of 'Crisis talks in fight to stem migrant hordes' and discussed the 'amnesty' (*Express* 2, 3 June 2011). Nigel Farage from UKIP was quoted:

> The message we are sending to the rest of the world is: Come on down, Britain is a soft touch. You can come here illegally and it doesn't matter, no-one's going to bother and after a few years you'll be given full rights to stay.
>
> (*Express* 2, 3 June 2011)

This message was reinforced later in the article:

> Many more migrants are now waiting in illegal camps around Calais, which they use as a springboard to get into Britain. All play a cat and mouse game with the police, jumping on trains and lorries for an illegal passage to Dover.
>
> (*Express* 2, 3 June 2011)

An alternative view was aired in *The Times*. A letter from the head of public policy at the Red Cross, George McNamara, said that asylum seekers must not be refused simply because of a concern over their numbers, but that each case must be considered on its merits. He stressed that 'we should not blame those caught up in the asylum backlog for the shortcomings of the system' (*The Times* 2, 3 June 2011).

The Benefits of Immigration

In the Press

Given that it was World Refugee Week from 20–26 June, there was a notable lack of positive stories about asylum seekers in June 2011. The benefits of immigration in general were mentioned in only three articles, discussing asylum (or asylum alongside economic migration) in the 2011 sample of 69, in the *Daily Mail* and *The Times*. The *Daily Mail* allowed that 'Yes, immigration has brought some benefits to this country', but this qualified an article attacking 'a back door amnesty' and detailing the Conservative failure to 'end Labour's policy of open door immigration' (*Daily Mail* 2, 3 June 2011). A piece in the *Express* in contrast directly argued against the United Kingdom being a historically diverse nation, and dismissed as 'deceitful propaganda' what it called 'the false claim that immigration has boosted our economy' (*Express* 1, 13 June 2011).

In wider debate we found examples in the *Guardian* (10 June 2011) and the *Mirror* of articles citing British Chamber of Commerce claims that measures to tighten economic migration would be disruptive 'to economic recovery' (*Mirror*, 10 June 2011). The notion of asylum seekers or refugees benefiting Britain is rarely found. In the *Guardian*, a letter was published from several refugee groups commemorating World Refugee Day. It paid:

> tribute to the refugees who have made enormous contributions to British society. From the invention of the iconic Mini to the birth of some of the world's most successful businesses, refugees have made their mark in the worlds of commerce, science, politics and the arts.
>
> (*Guardian*, 20 June 2011)

A positive story was included in the *Guardian* more recently, a first-person account by Latefa Guemar, an Algerian refugee in Britain who is now studying for her PhD: 'My hope is to contribute to this county – if I'm given the opportunity' (31 August 2012). Intriguingly, in the latest British Social Attitudes survey, those who believed immigration had positively benefited Britain had risen: 'to around 30%, up from 26% in 2002. But then, so has the number who believe the impact has been "very bad" – almost doubled from 11 to 21%' (Rogers, 2012). These statistics are likely to be a reflection of the heightened debate and concern in public consciousness over the potential economic 'burdens' or 'benefits' of immigration and asylum issues that has accompanied the economic crisis in recent years.

Problems Facing Asylum Seekers

On TV News

There were three TV news items that included interviews with asylum seekers and refugees (four speakers in total), and they all referred to hardships they had faced. The first interviewee on ITV *News at Ten* was Fis Bellingim from Sri Lanka. As noted above, the programme did not say why he had fled the country, and although he was an asylum seeker who had waited eight years then been granted permission to stay, he was not described as a refugee. He was not asked why he sought asylum, but instead, 'Why did you come to this country?' His answer via an interpreter was that 'This country people say is granting asylum, that's why I came here.'

Forfana from Sierra Leone, the second interviewee on ITV *News at Ten*, described why many asylum seekers 'go underground': 'they are scared to appear. Because they scared you they say if we hold you, you go to prison.' Forfana, was said to 'not want to be identified' and his face was blurred. As no wider context was given of why asylum seekers might fear detention and the possibility and consequences of deportation to their home country, his account implied only a fear of 'getting caught'. This was followed (see page 97) by the election poster, '"We don't know how many illegal immigrants there are but they're welcome to stay. And bring a mate." LibDem Manifesto 2010' (ITV *News at Ten*, 2 June 2011).

More context on the reasons refugees leave their homes was

given in the *Channel 4 News* that featured Barbek Mohammed. The voiceover introduced him as he entered his business, a barbershop: 'Barbek Mohammed fled war-torn Afghanistan for Britain nearly a decade ago. For years he tried to persuade the authorities to grant him asylum here, and for years he failed' (*Channel 4 News*, 2 June 2011). Mohammed was referred to as a 'former asylum seeker'. The programme, though it described him as having 'fled war-torn Afghanistan', stopped short of calling him a refugee, the correct term for an asylum seeker who has been given leave to remain. This implied that a question mark still hung over his status, though legally it does not. The presenter claimed that 'then quite suddenly last year he was told he can stay'. Barbek told the interviewer how happy he was. The voiceover to footage of him working was, 'He now runs two busy hairdressers and hopes to save enough money to bring his wife and children here.'

ITV *Lunchtime News* also gave some context to Whaid's story. He was interviewed in a Refugee Council Advice and Day Centre which was described as helping around 200 people a day, 'asylum seekers dropping in for food, lessons and advice on how to deal with their immigration status'. A voiceover began, 'Whaid, who doesn't want to show his face, has been here for six years. A political protester in Iran, he fled in fear of his life. He lives in limbo, not knowing if he can stay here permanently' (ITV *Lunchtime News*, 2 June 2011). This was the only programme that highlighted the impact on vulnerable people forced to wait many years for a decision. Whaid explained how happy he would be to be able to work and support himself 'like normal people'. The images used in this feature emphasized numbers, but one of queues of men waiting showed one man lifting up a small child at his feet. This was a more sympathetic image than the crowds prominent in other coverage. The piece on Whaid was followed by an interview with Damian Green, in the presenter commented that some people have 'made a real *mockery* of those men and women who *genuinely* live in fear of their lives'. Green agreed, saying that 'among the people who suffer are genuine refugees'. As he commented:

> One of the advantages of getting the system back under control, as we are now increasingly doing, is that we can take decisions quickly so that those who are genuine refugees can be allowed to get on with their

lives, and those who have no right to remain here can be removed from the country. Only yesterday, I opened a new detention centre, which means we've got a lot more places available, which will make it easier for us to remove people who have no right to be here.

(ITV *Lunchtime News*, 2 June 2011)

This concluded the report and was not questioned by the presenter. There was no suggestion here or elsewhere in the news report that the systems of 'immigration control' and detention might also present difficulties and hardship for 'genuine refugees'.

The TV coverage was dominated by government voices. The strongest voice was Green's: he featured in all the programmes. David Cameron was shown twice (ITV *Evening News*, 2 June 2011 and BBC1 *10 O'Clock News*, 2 June 2011), and Nick Clegg was shown once (*Channel 4 News*, 2 June 2011), both of them in clips from 2010 election coverage. Keith Vaz spoke on all but BBC1 *10 O'Clock News* (2 June 2011), and was the only opposition voice. There was also a comment by an academic from the Oxford Migration Observatory.

We should also note a *Panorama* programme broadcast at this time, 'Breaking into Britain' (BBC, 2011). Despite the tabloid overtones of the title, the programme and the subsequent online commentary by Evan Davis attempted to tell the stories of 'migrants' from their own perspective. In his commentary, Davis described being at Calais and witnessing young men apparently from Afghanistan, attempting to climb onto trucks bound for Britain. But he then humanised their experience by focusing on the fear of a young boy:

For me, any thoughts of disapproval at the unruly behaviour I was witnessing evaporated at the sight of a teenage boy cowering danger-ously at the top of a lorry driver's cab under the back canopy. He was not a trouble-maker. He was obviously petrified but still so desperate to get on to a car ferry to Britain, he was going to take the risk.

(BBC, 2011)

This differed greatly from other media coverage, which has presented the 'invasion' merely as a threat, and which so imprinted the images of Sangatte on public memory. Davis spoke of the terrible conditions under which people travel and are received:

Perhaps the saddest revelation was the indecency of the reception in the European Union. It is in Greece that many Afghan migrants' illusions of Europe as a welcoming place are quickly shattered. Many have run out of money and find themselves sleeping rough on the streets of Athens with no hope of moving on to western Europe .... They tell of being extorted at every turn, by passport control at borders and police along the way to people smugglers demanding thousands to take them on the dangerous lorry trip across the Sahara desert to Morocco.

(BBC, 2011)

And he described the dangers faced by women on these journeys:

For the women who have risked everything, the dangers are even more grave. They described to Kassim the smugglers who demand sex in exchange for their passage, even if they have already paid for their trip. Many make it no further than the brothels of Africa.

(BBC, 2011)

This was clearly very sympathetic to the plight of the individuals concerned, though the distinction between economic migrants and refugees was still not made clear. In one sense of course they are all human beings, and that sense of humanity was carried through the commentary. But it is the case that if people are 'fleeing violence' as Davis describes, they can potentially claim asylum and are not economic migrants. There is also of course the issue of to what extent the West bears some responsibility for the conflicts from which people are fleeing. That said, this is clearly an important counter-example to much of the coverage we have analysed, which presented 'floods' of refugees merely as a threat.

In the Press

In the press coverage, problems facing migrants were mentioned in 12 articles out of the 69 which discussed asylum seekers (or asylum alongside economic migration) in the sample. Five of these references were in the *Guardian*, and two in the *Telegraph*. In one example from the *Guardian*, a woman now seeking asylum described having been abused and enslaved by her employer in the United Kingdom, a diplomat, leading to threats against her in her home country which meant she could not return there (28 June 2011). A letter, also in the *Guardian*. from a member of Student Action for Refugees stressed the difficulty faced by asylum seekers who seek to gain an education and find they are 'called international students and charged huge fees'. It argues that 'access to university should be based on academic achievement, not whether the Home Office has managed to assess an asylum claim' (*Guardian* 2, 2 June 2011). The paper also took up the case of a rejected asylum seeker who faced deportation to Nigeria before an ongoing investigation into the claim she had been raped in Britain was concluded. Her case had been 'fast-tracked', a process intended for straightforward cases, and the paper described how she was being kept on 'suicide watch' (*Guardian*, 22 June 2011).

Single references were found to this theme in *The Times* and the *Express*, which described conditions in squats in Calais where police raids were 'a daily occurrence, with complaints that beatings are common and that water is poured over blankets and food'. This long article also called for stricter border controls to 'stem migrant hordes' (*Express* 2, 3 June 2011). The *Sun* also carried a letter which said, 'The refugees in Glasgow's Red Road flats feel isolated and cut off from society' (*Sun* 2, 15 June 2011). The *Daily Mail,* in an article referred to above, described the 'Voodoo terror of teen girls brought to UK as sex slaves' (*Daily Mail* 2, 23 June 2011). The paper elsewhere briefly gave voice to an asylum seeker who was subjected to 'degrading treatment' in being returned to Greece, but the thrust of the argument was that those fleeing the 'Arab Spring' were driven by financial gain (*Daily Mail* 1, 23 June 2011). The main point, as we have noted, was that a change in the rules to disallow returns to countries like Greece would leave 'Britain vulnerable to a new influx of migrants' (*Daily Mail* 1, 23 June 2011).

In contrast to sympathetic references, in other tabloid articles (such as the *Sun*'s 'Migrant luxury', *Sun* 2, 2 June 2011, quoted above), detention centres were described as unduly opulent. The *Daily Mail* also described 'lawns with Greek statues' and quoted the Taxpayers Alliance saying costs 'need to be kept under control' as 'Immigration Centres are for people who have no right to be in the UK' (*Daily Mail* 1, 2 June 2011). Conservative MP James Clappison was quoted criticising the cost of the centre: 'people should be treated decently and humanely but at a time of public spending constraint that should not extend as far as standards that are beyond the reach of ordinary taxpayers' (*Daily Mail* 1, 2 June 2011). This article claimed that 'New arrivals will be greeted by impressive lawns and extensive gardens, patrolled by a flock of ducks' (*Daily Mail* 1, 2 June 2011).

These references were to Morton Hall, in which people were seen being frisked in the *Channel 4 News* broadcast. It was shown as a hostile backdrop in much of the TV sample discussed above. In the *Daily Mail* article there was no mention of the queues of people, cells, security guards, doors, high mesh fences and steel gates that featured in much of the TV footage. Three detainees attempted or threatened to jump from the roof of this centre in 2012 because of the conditions there and their prolonged detention (Van Steenburgen, 2012). The phrase 'No right to be here/in UK' appeared three times in the article (*Daily Mail* 1, 2 June 2011), yet there is of course, a right for those who fear persecution to claim asylum, and there is no law against claiming asylum and having the claim rejected.

In July, sympathy in all the papers grew for the situation in Somalia. For example *Daily Mail*: 9 July 2011; *Mirror*: 11–12 July 2011; and *Sun* 1: 11–12 July 2011 were articles about refugees fleeing the Somalian drought and conflict. The *Mirror* in particular took up the cause and stressed 'violence every day', echoing the United Nations on the need for western intervention as 'camps can't handle the millions hit by drought' (*Mirror*, 11 July 2011). This same article quoted one refugee, Abdi Hassan: 'There was already violence every day in Somalia, and the drought has made it worse.' This coverage focused on aid for refugees in mainland Africa, however, not support for those seeking asylum in the United Kingdom.

On the same day the *Sun* included a story criticising the amount spent on legal aid for five asylum seekers claiming compensation after their refugee status papers were delayed for between seven and ten months, keeping them in hardship and without rights to work and be treated as full UK citizens. The article, called '£110k asylum rap' stated that 'Judges have blasted a compensation claim made by five asylum seekers under the Human Rights Act which cost taxpayers more than £110,000' (*Sun* 2, 11 July 2011). A similar but more extensive story appeared in the *Daily Mail*. Once again the focus was not on the asylum seekers' hardship, but what the paper described as the wasteful pursuit of compensation under the Human Rights Act:

> Five asylum seekers took the Home Office to court over a delay in issuing documents which would allow them to claim benefits and work legally. They carried on with their legal action, dragging it out for over a year, even after the correct paperwork was issued and officials apologised.
>
> (*Daily Mail*, 10 July 2011)

The theme of problems faced by those seeking asylum most often featured in *Guardian* coverage. During June there were a relatively small number of articles in this paper dealing with asylum. In July the paper produced a number of articles in this category, including one with the headline 'Amnesty urges complete overhaul of deportation process: failed asylum seekers "beaten and strangled". Firms accused of failing to train guards properly' (7 July 2011). Another reported condemnation of the immigration authorities' practice of taking detainees to the airport as 'reserves' for others being deported as 'inhumane' (*Guardian*, 26 July 2011). An article that included the voices of both a refugee and a refugee rights group revealed that child detention in asylum cases 'never quite went away, and is now making a comeback' (*Guardian*, 28 July 2011).

More recent articles have highlighted the destitution experienced by refugees, as in the case of a mother and baby who died in October 2012: 'A baby boy starved to death in Westminster as his seriously ill and "socially isolated" mother struggled to obtain proper housing, benefits and support, a serious case review into his death has revealed' (*Guardian*, 5 October 2012). According to the article, the problem was in the transition from NASS to mainstream benefits. The *Guardian* went on to say, 'The family had become "destitute" because of the withdrawal of the service's support ... and were being given cash handouts by healthcare workers and social services "to tide them over".' In the media as a whole such commentary is rare, as are the voices of refugees themselves, an issue we discuss more extensively below in our interviews and focus groups.

The Role of the West in Refugee Movements
and Economic Forces in Migration

In the Press

In our June 2011 sample we found no examples of stories which discussed the West's complicity or responsibility in relation to forced migration. We did however find one in the *Guardian* the following month, just outside our sample period, entitled 'Famine we could avoid: to pin the Somalia crisis on drought is wrong. This is an entirely predictable, man-made calamity' (*Guardian*, 22 July 2011). The article explained how the drought was the result of climate change, a human-induced disaster, and the effects of 'mainstream national development' pursued by governments. This had 'marginalised and discriminated against' traditional pastoralists despite their methods being more productive (*Guardian*, 22 July 2011). The impacts of poverty and drought had been made worse by the effects of the war, which had left people vulnerable and without resources to survive it. The article also stressed that 'Somalia has been made a war zone by the US-led "war on terror"' (*Guardian*, 22 July 2011).

There was some alternative reporting of the crisis of refugees fleeing the Arab Spring in an article again just outside our sample. An article drawn from the *Independent* the previous month contrasted with the support given to David Cameron and Theresa May rejecting EU plans and sending asylum seekers back to countries of 'first entry'. It acknowledged the United Kingdom as sharing some responsibility for those displaced by the Arab Spring conflicts stating that, 'Britain and France have been criticised for intervening in Libya but refusing to take refugees from the conflict there' (*Independent*, 23 May 2011).

The overall lack of such arguments in the bulk of the mainstream media means migration and refugee flows are routinely presented only in terms of narrow UK national interests. But discussions of global trends and foreign and economic policies are inseparable from migration issues, and media inclusion of these should help to provide a fuller understanding.

Overall in the period of this study we can see a decline in the frequency and relative profile of news items on the issues of asylum and refugees. A search on the number of newspaper articles referring to 'asylum seekers' showed a total for 2006 of 1,961.[3] This fell to 1,351 for the whole of 2011 and 547 for the first eight months of 2012. This is perhaps because by 2012 the media, especially the tabloids, had found new folk devils to attack: for example people on incapacity or other benefits (Briant, Watson and Philo, 2011). Migration remained an issue in 2013 with the predicted arrival of people from Bulgaria and Romania, under provisions within the European Union, but the emphasis has shifted somewhat from asylum seekers.

Even a potentially major story such as the death of Jimmy Mubenga and the subsequent debate in Parliament about the conduct of Border Agency staff received relatively muted coverage (Quakers Asylum and Refugee Network, 2012). There was coverage in some of the broadsheets and online editions, but it was not covered on national television news on the BBC or Channel 4 between 17 and 23 July. The focus had moved elsewhere, and as we have seen, there is little appetite in the national media as a whole for stories that promote the cause for asylum seekers.

---

3   Based on a search in the newspaper database 'newsbank' for the *Guardian*, the *Telegraph*, *The Times*, the *Sun*, the *Daily Mail*, the *Mirror* and the *Express*.

5

Impacts of Media Coverage on Migrant Communities in the United Kingdom

For this part of the study we interviewed a series of focus groups with four or five members. Each group was comprised of people from either the Asian or Afro-Caribbean communities. We asked five questions which the group members answered in writing, and which then formed the basis for subsequent discussion. In some cases we also conducted telephone interviews to clarify or elaborate upon earlier answers. The questions we asked were:

1 What image or thought comes to your mind when you hear the words 'refugee' or 'asylum seeker'?
2 Write a news headline from your own memory about refugees or asylum seekers.
3 Do you think that media coverage has affected how people in the UK think about refugees and asylum seekers? If so, how?
4 Has this affected anyone you know, including yourself?
5 Has such coverage affected your community as a whole, and how others see it?

For question 2, the group members wrote their own news headlines (see page 52). As we noted earlier, only one of the headlines they produced had any reference to a sympathetic portrayal of asylum seekers or refugees: it described them as 'vulnerable'. All of the other headlines focused on issues such as numbers and criminality, or used words such as 'flood'. When the groups actually discussed the issues, there were very varied responses, some of which were sympathetic, others more hostile. There were also very extensive discussions, particularly in the Asian groups, about the impact of the coverage on their own communities.

We will divide discussion of the answers into three main areas. The first involves the attitudes and responses when people were asked to think about issues involving asylum and refugees. Second are the specific impacts of media coverage on belief and understanding, and third are the effects of coverage on local established migrant communities.

In answers to the first question, there was some hostility expressed, partly on the grounds of whether all asylum seekers were 'genuine' refugees and also because of perceived pressures in local areas on housing and transport. It was asserted for example that refugees took priority in housing. No specific evidence was given of this, but it remained as a generalised belief in some group members. As one put it:

> [Refugees] walk in here and you may be struggling but you get a place to live and it's very difficult but I find the way refugees come in ... and [refugees] are there with a supermarket trolley and are then begging in the early hours. This is not all refugees but some of them. They get help in this country, you pay for their help but you can't get help, you are told you're not priority enough to get a house.
>
> (British Afro-Caribbean male)

There were also references to what were seen as criminal acts and bad behaviour associated with 'refugee' groups. In another group, a woman expressed the immediate negative connotations that the word refugee had for her:

> When I think of these things, the negative always overlooks the positive because it scares you more and then you feel like, why have these people come here, why have they been allowed to come here, and if the government have allowed them in, then why aren't they controlling them? Like if you're coming to this area then you have to think twice because you're scared because of all the stories you hear and everything.
>
> (British Asian female)

In another group, a man commented on the 'influx' into the area and its effect on crime:

> If you look at our local areas, there's a huge influx and there's quite a lot of crime, I would say, in the area.
>
> (British Asian male)

The moderator then asked whether the people referred to were actually refugees. It is apparent from the reply that the people the man was referring to were from Europe:

> I don't know exactly who they are and what they are, all we know is that there has been an influx to the area of people who are arriving from European countries and you just think they're creating a lot of trouble.
>
> (British Asian male)

The people were then described as 'gypsies from Romania'. People from Romania are not refugees but are free to move to the United Kingdom under the provisions of the European Union treaties. But the important issue here is how the words 'refugees' and 'asylum seeker' become generic terms for what is perceived as bad behaviour by new groups of people.

To pursue this further, the moderator then asked the group:

> *Moderator*: When you thought of the Romanians, you thought of them as asylum seekers and refugees when they weren't ... Why would they be called refugees?
> *Male 1*: Because they are trying to get onto the benefit ladder.
> *Moderator*: That might be, if they were just called 'economic migrants' or 'people from Eastern Europe'. As soon as I said 'refugees', 'asylum seekers', you put them into that category. So why?
> *Female 2*: I think it's the way they behave, hanging around street corners.
> *Moderator*: Do you have in your head an idea of how refugees behave?
> *Female 2*: Yeah, just hanging around street corners, hanging around in big gangs ...

The source of this association was then revealed as being media images of 'refugees in Calais':

> *Male 1*: If you look at the media and the news coverage, what you see

every day, more or less every second or third day, what you see they show you this many refugees tried to get on a truck from Calais to come over and they have all been staying in this jungle, for the last two months and they have been living rough. Then they show you Germany and the refugees there, all standing around on street corners. The pictures come from there and then you think that's what's going to happen when they get to this country.

This suggests a very powerful link between media representations and audience belief. The groups then went on to explore how media images can create such negative perceptions.

Media Images and Impacts on Public Understanding

The arrival of new groups to a stratified society, whether they are poor economic migrants or destitute refugees, can put pressure on the poorest areas of that society where there are already scarce resources in health, housing and education. The media can respond in several different ways to this. Newspapers, magazines and TV programmes could focus on the plight of the new arrivals and pressurise policy makers to respond to the needs of refugees or other groups by directing appropriate resources and reducing the stress in local areas. Alternatively they could exploit the potential tensions for their own commercial advantage. We have shown above which direction the bulk of the media took in relation to their presentation of asylum and refugees. There was a clear sense expressed by some in the groups of the pressures in local areas, as in these comments about the difficulties of finding work:

Well, basically, like in London now, for instance, and I'm talking now. I don't have a job now. I was made redundant three months ago and I'm looking for another one. I've been here 23 years and I've never ... well, I've been made redundant before but when I was made redundant in the past, it was more from one job to the other. I get a job straight away, in two or three weeks. Now it's taking me several months and I'm still looking basically, so basically those people are coming in, they put pressure on the available jobs basically, so if you let them in the country, that means that the people who live in the country will not get jobs much faster.

(Afro-Caribbean male)

The numbers of people migrating and the role of the media in highlighting this were consistent themes:

> The media is making us more aware of these people and who is being allowed in the country. When the media is pointing out there is X amount of people from X amount of countries you start to notice it around you.
>
> (British Asian female)

But there was also sympathy expressed. An Asian male spoke of asylum seekers as 'our brothers and sisters', and an Afro-Caribbean woman spoke of their vulnerability in this exchange about the first thing that came into her head when she thought of them:

> *Female 1*: The first thing? I think ... desperate but I don't want to use the word desperate, hopeless.
> *Moderator*: You mean people who are in need of support ... that need your help?
> *Female 1*: Yes.

There was extensive discussion in the groups about the manner in which media portrayals operated to construct negative accounts of refugees and asylum. A key issue raised was how hostile media stories prey upon the fears of existing communities and 'stir them' by consistent negative portrayals:

> I think the way the media portrays asylum seeking is never positive, but there are positive effects of people coming into this country and their contribution to the economy but never ever do you hear a positive side, it's always a negative side because they are preying on people's fears and that's what's going to grab headlines.
>
> (British Asian male)

A second speaker in the same group then commented on how a single instance involving a family from Afghanistan had been inflated in the press to create a climate of hostility:

> I was reading an article about an Afghani family who were claiming housing benefit. They weren't actually committing any benefit fraud and were being paid by the local authority but because the amount was really high, as it was in London, but it was shown up just because they

were of a certain nationality which had no relevance to what they were doing. That to me is an example of the kind of coverage that the media has been doing for the last ten years or so, since the whole asylum thing started. It's taking an issue and making it more emotive by putting in nationality and a slant on it to say it is terrible to say that these folk coming from abroad and stealing our resources and taking our benefits away from our own people. This constant opinion put through by the media into the public domain fuels people's emotions.

(British Asian male)

The crucial issue that he raised is how a culture of belief and false generalisations without evidence becomes pervasive in everyday conversation.

In another group the discussion also focused on how the media concentrate on negative issues, leaving out anything positive. In this case, some in the group distinguished between a small number of middle-class women from Pakistan whom they believed were not 'legitimate' refugees, and people from Afghanistan and other areas whom they saw as being more in need. This local experience of seeing people arrive was then combined in their accounts with their description of the impact of media images, with one saying they made her 'feel bitter':

> *Male 1*: The media doesn't throw in our faces that this is what this asylum seeker has done, or a group of them have done which is a positive aspect. You don't see that side of it, you only see it as negative, or it is not there.
> *Female 1*: Exactly, because the only thing we see is that is soon as these people are a burden on the economy and as soon as they get leave to remain, they just get bombarded with all these benefits and the taxpayer, we're just like, it gets annoying.
> *Male 2*: They do show on TV that these people moving into some areas, I think it was Birmingham, and got brand new flats and furniture and there were riots there because some people are living on the same estate and some never got them.
> *Female 1*: Yeah, you do feel bitter.
>
> (British Asians)

Some in the groups pointed to specific newspapers or TV programmes associated with very negative coverage. The programme *UK Border Force* was referred to by this participant as offering a simple good and bad vision of the world, with nothing heard from people seeking asylum:

> [On] *UK Border Force*, you'll see the good versus the bad and you'll see the immigration officers taking action by pulling them out of vans and trucks but you never hear of the personal account from an asylum seeker, you'll never hear what they've been through to get here.
>
> (British Asian male)

The key omission was of any sustained commentary from the asylum seekers and refugees themselves. This was pointed to by members of these groups, as one noted:

> The media is always negative. They are never going to do a story that says a refugee came over and started a successful business and employed so many people.
>
> (British Asian male)

Another commented on the absence of the desperate and tragic stories of some refugees which he has heard himself but not seen in the media:

> You can form an emotional connection. They sit down and tell you their story: 'I was sat in the back of a truck for 12 hours, then this happened to my kids and I got beaten up there and that was our journey,' and you listen to people. I've met asylum seekers in mosques around here and spoken to them, you know, like 'What's your journey, what happened?' We've had people who have worked for us in the same situation and it's the same stories, you're just horrified. That's what you've got and you're the same age as me. I've never seen that in the media, never seen that covered.
>
> (British Asian male)

Another participant in the groups pointed to the impacts that negative media coverage had on beliefs and attitudes in his own community. He also saw this as a major failure in the responsibility of government:

> The media play on bias and make it worse to stir it up because that's how they make headlines, that's making things racially worse. They know what they are doing and the government knows what they are doing, but the government is doing nothing to stop it. Where is the

watchdog on this? Where is a media watchdog? I think the government might even be planting stories to be honest, not directly but they're not stopping stories that they should be stopping…. These negative things affect us, even if they are our own brothers and sisters. Just imagine how it affects white people. I don't know why it isn't stopped, there should be some sort of censor in the media to stop this kind of racially charged stories. Like I said, it's passive racism.

(British Asian male)

Another major issue discussed by people in these groups was how the intertwining of media pressures and government policy had impacts on their community as a whole, and specifically on their sense of identity and security.

Impacts of Media Coverage on Established
Migrant Groups and Descendants

There was a belief among some in the groups that the negative media coverage affected them because it was essentially racially based and their whole community was judged as being under suspicion. This was felt especially by Asian groups, and was also related by some to Islamophobia in the wake of the 9/11 attacks. Government and media attitudes to migration and to the pressure that was put on asylum seekers were central to the experience of some in the groups. As one put it, in the eyes of the public, everyone in his community was treated as basically the same:

> Everything is linked in a way. I feel negative views start from [the media] but then we are all in the same boat because we are from the same origin. Doesn't matter if we were born here or whatever, in the public view, the Joe Bloggs view, we are all basically the same. On the street, guys walk by, they can't tell what's what; they'll put me in the same boat as asylum seekers. Why should I have to prove I'm not an asylum seeker? I work in a shop right now and I know what most people think, they think of us all in the same light until we prove ourselves, but why should we have to prove it?

(British Asian male)

Another pointed to the impact of the arrival of asylum seekers and how this gave him a 'promotion' from his original status, since now there was another group below him that could be abused:

When asylum seekers came to Glasgow I felt I had got a promotion, I felt I was promoted even though I was born in Glasgow, from being racially beaten up, abused, marginalised for most of my life. When asylum seekers first came to Glasgow, I was now seen as Glaswegian. [There was a boy who said] 'You're all right now but I don't like these new folk.' I had suddenly been promoted from the bottom rung to the next rung. He said 'now' because there was a new group of people who could be marginalised and to bully.

(British Asian male)

As with the previous speaker, he felt the pressure to distinguish himself from the newly arrived asylum seekers:

The thing is, sometimes when I'm speaking to people, I feel pressured to speak with a greater Glaswegian accent so they don't ask questions like where I'm from or if I just came here yesterday.

(British Asian male)

The pressure was felt especially by people who ran businesses and who saw themselves as on the front line of attacks by the government, police and migration authorities. One woman said that although she was a British citizen and owned a shop, she still felt that she had to carry her passport with her all the time in case she was picked up in the raids that took place in her area.

This is an important dimension to the impact of government policy and media coverage in relation to migration and asylum – that it has created fear and destabilised existing communities apart from its immediate and draconian effects on actual refugees and asylum seekers. The participant who spoke of carrying her passport described the fear generated as people were rounded up and put in vans, while another described how customers had been thrown out of a restaurant:

Female 1: Six or seven months ago the police were coming in vans and running out into shops and people hiding in bathrooms and then they were rounding them up and putting them in vans. That was scary because how can you tell which one of us is an asylum seeker and which ones are genuinely here? We're all assimilated now so you can't really tell. It's affected me a lot because I grew up in London and all you learn about in history is about the Nazis and Jews and what happened to them in the 1930s, and it was scenes like that happening...
Male 1: The restaurant beside me, on a Saturday evening they just

come in and just throw everyone out. It doesn't matter how many there are eating, they just get thrown out. So he's lost all that money from customers too.

(British Asians)

Another participant who described how he was born and raised in Britain described the raids on his own shops:

I've been raided about five times, when I've been working in my own shops. The way they treat you, that's the worst bit, it's like you're the criminal.

(British Asian male)

There were also references to the impact of media images in spreading anxiety:

Female 1: On TV, they show raids at 5 or 6 o'clock in the morning, they show the police battering the door and running into the house...
Female 2: What I think is, how can they differentiate between me and an asylum seeker?

(British Asians)

And the effect of a programme such as *UK Border Force* was again discussed:

Male 1: There seems to be a lot of public demand to know about this subject, I mean you see programmes like *UK Border Force* ... It's 'good versus bad', that's what they are pushing.
Male 2: It emotionally affects you; it puts worry in your mind.

(British Asians)

Some participants made the point very strongly that the effect of the attacks was to undermine their own rights and their identity as British citizens:

Female 1: It's the way Scottish people look at you as well, isn't it? OK, there are asylum seekers, but they look at us when we go out.
Male 1: Yeah, and label us. Things have changed and the media is the biggest blame to put on it. Never before did people like us get questioned. We wouldn't get stopped on the road but now your car gets stopped and [you are] asked what are you doing out at this time of the night?

(British Asians)

The last participant then went on to describe a specific encounter with the police:

> *Male 1*: The question that annoyed me the most was [when] he said, 'Where are you from?' and I said, 'Well, could you clear the question?' He said, 'Where were you born?' I said, 'Ealing, in London.' Then he said, 'But where are you from?' I said, 'I'm from London.' He goes, 'No, then what's your ethnic background?' I said, 'I'm British or Scottish.' I knew where he was coming from.
>
> (British Asian)

The moderator then asked if the issue here was of 'identity, ethnicity and whether you are "really" British?':

> *Male 1*: Yes, that's it.
> *Female 1*: Exactly.
> *Male 1*: He turned over and there's a pink page and he says, 'British ethnic'; Indian-Asian, Pakistani-Asian and all that. He said, 'Which group do you belong to?' I said, 'To be honest none of them because I'm a British Asian.' He said, 'No, you have to tick one of these boxes.' And [he carried on] until it turned out I was Pakistani, which I'm not. I was born in this country so I count myself as British, I don't count myself as Pakistani. I've got the same rights as everybody else; I pay the same amount of tax and do everything else, so why should I have to be labelled? That's what's causing major problems.
>
> (British Asians)

This man's conclusion was that 'the media stir it and label everyone the same!' The creation of this climate of fear and the impact on established communities is a product in part of media coverage and the interaction of this with the activities of government, police and migration authorities. The impacts are of course felt most severely by refugees themselves, and in the next section we discuss the results of interviews with them and professional workers in the area.

Impacts of Media Coverage on Asylum-Seeking Communities

Discussions of Media Coverage

In our analysis of the impact of coverage we conducted 36 interviews with asylum seekers, refugees, refugee workers and other professionals with particular knowledge and experience of asylum issues. We asked first about their own views on media coverage, and second, discussed the impact of television and press coverage on the lives of refugees and asylum seekers, and the communities in which they live. Overall there was concern about the levels of hostile coverage of asylum issues, and its confusion with 'illegal immigration'. An interviewee argued that 'we're talking about the media abusing a whole section of society ... just because it makes a story' (asylum worker). Issues were raised by interviewees that reflected the same trends and problems revealed by our content analysis. These were seen as impacting on public understanding, with very negative consequences for refugees. However, some refugee workers did note improvement in recent years:

> I think it's getting better than it was a few years ago. Some years ago it was absolutely diabolical and asylum seemed to be a free for all for anyone who could say anything shocking about [asylum seekers] to get people to read their newspapers.
>
> (refugee worker)

Negative headlines in the press were often seen as more influential than positive coverage in for example TV current affairs. As a refugee services manager commented, 'It makes me want to read it with the shocking headlines, whereas things like *Dispatches* ... you only watch it if you want to' and are already concerned about asylum. However, a refugee services manager described the BBC's *Panorama* programme 'Breaking into Britain' (see pp. 124–5) as having a '*Daily Mail*-type' headline to 'attract all the audiences'. She said that by contrast the content was positive, and 'really powerful'.

The refugee workers suggested that media coverage should emphasise positive impacts, and these were not sufficiently shown. The interviewees stressed that society benefits greatly from its refugee population. One stated that:

> Glasgow benefited because most ... refugees, they're working so they are experienced. So [there are a] really very small proportion of people not working ... success stories are there.
>
> (refugee worker/Sri Lankan refugee)

He was keen to point out that 'We are contributing to society by – for example, my organisation, we are building a Robert Burns statue.' He stressed that this was 'our idea to do something for the city' which had given them so much. Several interviewees (including a refugee worker/Congolese refugee) pointed out that 'the diversity of the people who come' enriched British communities. One interviewee pointed to how 'We've seen the contribution for example ... with the Olympic Games' and 'the Mini-Cooper, which is a car designed by a refugee' and is 'now part of the British heritage' (refugee worker/ Congolese refugee).

The absence of any positive coverage of asylum was heavily criticised by our refugee sample. One asserted that:

> if TV start to say people more and more true information and ... show us a programme about asylum seekers who good integrate to the British community, who good educate their children here, who study in a colleges and universities, and they going to be good British community member, of course ... British people's opinion would be much ... better about asylum seekers.
>
> (asylum seeker, Russia)

Reports of local media coverage were mixed. Some people did not see local media as particularly focused on refugee issues. One joked that they just talk about 'sheep' (youth project worker). In one example, an interviewee argued that 'There no much coverage about the asylum seekers ... They forgotten a lot,' but, he said, 'they don't portray very badly asylum seekers' (refugee worker/Sri Lankan refugee). This same interviewee's organisation was donating the statue mentioned above to the city, and was getting coverage from the local paper that week.

Another interviewee observed that the way asylum and immigration generally are covered by the local media 'very much will depend on the population in that community', giving the example of their local area in which there are 'lots of Polish people and Lithuanian people'. In the local media 'comments from ... people within the council' had been 'a bit negative' and 'shocking' (youth project worker). Others said local media coverage gave a more balanced account, and gave refugees more of a voice. A refugee worker/Congolese refugee felt his local media were 'celebrating the diversity of Norfolk' and the contributions refugees made. One refugee services manager observed that 'any local press is more "human interest" ... unless of course it's a planning issue'. A refugee worker who is also a Congolese refugee reported having been featured in the local press several times, as well as in the *Guardian*.

Another interviewee observed that in Norwich:

> The local newspaper and the local radio are very positive and they go out of their way to cover stories of any events that we're doing or other agencies in the region are doing and to sort of show asylum and refugees in a very positive light.

(refugee worker)

This was seen as particularly true during Refugee Week, and the challenge was seen as extending interest throughout the year. 'If you're hearing negative stuff throughout the whole year, what difference is one week going to make?' asked a refugee services manager.

Conflation of Asylum Issues with 'Illegal Immigration'

The use of umbrella terms like 'foreigners' and 'illegal immigrants' to refer to both migrants and asylum seekers was universally criticised. One refugee worker observed that:

> The press slot all immigrants in together. So asylum seekers are seen as part of immigration, which I think, you know, [they are] *completely* outside. Under the Refugee Convention it shouldn't be part of it.

(refugee worker – original emphasis)

This was linked by some to language. One observed that 'The word "illegals" is quite often thrown in but I know it's not an accurate status' (adult literacy coordinator). A term particularly criticised was 'illegal asylum seekers', which carries the perception that 'they're pretending, they've come here really just to work' (youth project worker).

One asylum seeker said that the media:

> can't even explain they always criminalise them, you know. They can't let people, the community to understand what is called refugee but they use the word illegal immigrant, you know, to confuse people.

(asylum seeker, Somalia)

One Glasgow city councillor also commented on the representation of asylum seekers' 'illegal entry' as being 'illegal immigration' in the media, rather than representing this as people fleeing persecution:

> Other asylum issues are again the issue of illegal immigration via freight or train to gain access here, as if it's a form of illegality that you have to sneak in rather than gaining access in terms of fleeing torture or persecution.

Refugees particularly criticised terms like 'illegal immigrant', saying that the media:

> try to criminalise them using illegal immigrants, using 'They came into the country illegally.' You know [the] sort of language they use, you know, it's not even refugee, again it's 'illegal immigrants'.
>
> (asylum seeker, Somalia)

This refugee argued that the use of the term 'illegal immigrant' helped justify the use of power and immigration controls: 'when they say like that government will have more power to do whatever, you know, removing people'. Another refugee described the personal effect this language had on him:

> I didn't want to come here because I want to claim benefit or ... I had a very good job back home, I was in a very good position. So I did not want just to come here and ... benefit from the UK economy, no. That's the truth. The reality is that whenever my country is safer, I'll go back, and want to go back and I want to contribute to my country. And when I hear terms like that it makes me feel that I'm very devalued. I have no value at all. And what's called 'illegality', it's ... doing something not right. But I still believe that ... it was right for me to get protection, it was right for me to flee my country ... it was right for me to ... get somewhere safe to live, so that was why I did it. .... When people say no, *I'm* illegal in the country, it makes me very upset.
>
> (refugee worker/Congolese refugee – original emphasis)

According to one refugee worker the use of such language has impacts on public understanding:

> a lot of people therefore confuse ... all immigrants with asylum seekers .... Several people have ... said to me, 'Oh, are all your asylum seekers

from Eastern Europe'? You know, because there's obviously a great deal of confusion.

(refugee worker)

This parallels the findings of our focus groups above, where generalised accounts and images such as of Sangatte in Calais had led to the word 'refugees' becoming an unspecific negative term, which was then applied to people from Romania. The refugees with whom we spoke were particularly critical of the way in which media accounts presented them as coming to Britain for economic reasons. One stated that:

> They show the natives of the country we are coming here only because of economic problem. They show the asylum seeker as poor people coming for a better life; they don't understand this is people running to get a safe place. They say 'This is an illegal immigrant, they are coming here to get what you have, to get your job, to get your money, to get your house,' nothing else, and people they act negative to asylum seeker instead of welcoming them, show them, help them to be integrated. They insulted them and that is a problem, being isolated.

(asylum seeker, Rwanda)

One interviewee drew attention to problems in the widespread use of the term 'failed asylum seeker':

> If they use the term 'failed asylum seeker' that is [also] obscenity-like, because often applications are rejected in error or because they are not yet proven ... many of the people who've 'failed' asylum ... many of those who have been deported ... have faced persecution. Many have been disappeared. Many have been killed.

(refugee worker and refugee)

He said that 'the fact they have failed in the UK, does not mean that another country would not give them protection', and that this is why they do not want to return to their country of origin. Often they are 'traumatised' and 'they prefer to commit suicide'. Even the choice of the phrase 'asylum seeker' over 'refugee' was also said to be part of the construction of a negative media image:

> When people hear the word refugee you know there's a reaction there, there's a sympathy. Asylum seeker is a new term that's been invented

to disassociate all of that, which brings with it the connotations of bogus asylum seeker which gets used all the time, which gets used on the news.

(Member of the Scottish Parliament)

One refugee reported feeling that the term 'asylum seeker' was now a term of abuse:

It's like an abuse even. If someone wants to abuse you even if you're not an asylum seeker any more, just tell them you're asylum seeker, an abuse now because of the media. Because of the media, bogus, it's like calling you bogus because you eat food? I mean ... the word asylum seeker is the same as bogus.

(asylum seeker, Uganda)

'Immigration Control' and Numbers

There was concern over the emphasis on numbers of asylum seekers coming into the United Kingdom in the media. One interviewee for example echoed our research findings above, and stated that the TV gives the impression that a large proportion of refugees worldwide are coming to the United Kingdom, but 'actually Britain only hosts less than 3 per cent of the refugees and most refugees go to a neighbouring country in Africa or Asia'. He argued that 'they need to say why people are seeking asylum' and 'the origin of the wars ... what creates conflict?' (refugee worker/Congolese refugee).

TV was described in another interview as:

Exaggerating in terms of quantities and numbers of people arriving which is false, totally false, because I understand that at this precise moment we accept something like 2 per cent of the world's refugee population. I know for a fact that the large majority of refugees are lucky if they make it across the border.

(charity support officer)

The same interviewee described seeing this in the news, *Question Time* and 'prime-time documentaries'. Another interviewee stated that on *Newsnight* the line was that 'there's too many coming in' (media development officer). Views of the language used by the TV coverage also emerged, as people described what they saw on TV. For example, 'There was instances with people coming into different ports, flooding the areas, taking all the resources' (lecturer). The images associated with this theme also appeared to be powerful, as in one account by a Glasgow city councillor:

> The two things that stand out in my mind is the French asylum centre, the holding centre just before Calais, Sangatte and literally thousands ... milling about there but trying to leave there, trying to make their way by train, freight, or whatever to Britain.
>
> (Glasgow city councillor)

One interviewee commented that the TV's focus was on controlling these numbers, through 'immigration control' and legal changes:

> They are talking all about laws always. They're changing that law and this law but always the publicity, the positive stories [positive from the Government perspective]. They cover up everything.
>
> (refugee worker/Sri Lankan refugee)

Another interviewee argued that the press more often focus on numbers, 'be that financial numbers or numbers coming in' (refugee services manager). TV by comparison could offer in-depth analysis, although it did not cover asylum often enough. She said:

> in the press it's all very negative, it's all money-based. You don't get the journey, you don't get an understanding of the whole picture. You only get finance [unclear] and ... exploitation and just the negatives but it's only a small picture of what goes on. You're not actually getting the history of a person.
>
> (refugee services manager)

This reiterates the point made in the focus groups that the voices of refugees, their history and personal experience, are passed over in most media accounts.

The 'Burden', Crime and Fear

The portrayal of asylum seekers as a burden was heavily criticised in the interviews. As one interviewee noted:

> I never hear anything positive about them or anything constructive

happening. Regarding them it's all about containment or deportation. They're seen as scavengers and thieves.

(youth project co-ordinator)

A youth project worker commented that:

some papers will give the opinion that there's many asylum seekers in this country who are sponging off the system and it's costing taxpayers money.

The *Guardian* was seen as a contrast to such coverage, focusing more on issues such as the treatment of asylum seekers in detention (according to a youth project worker). Other interviewees complained about the focus of the media on refugees as a burden, one saying:

[People] think they have money, everything, but person don't have food.

(refugee worker/Sri Lankan refugee)

A key absence was:

What's happening in other human beings' lives. Like, Glasgow there lot of people ... eating in soup kitchen, living in a shelter and when the summer comes they don't have any opportunity to have a – shelter is closed and they don't have a place. They sleeping rough, it's happening in Glasgow. This news they don't make [it into the] news.

(refugee worker/Sri Lankan refugee)

From the interviewee's experience working at the Red Cross centre in Glasgow, there are:

Hundreds and hundreds ... my experience, it's close a thousand people here .... No one want to talk about that.

(refugee worker/Sri Lankan refugee)

This leads to a lack of understanding of issues such as dependence on the state. One interviewee commented:

They always tell people they are taking our benefit, they are taking your houses, they are taking fridge, they are taking free water, free electricity, free this, free that, but they don't let people know the reality. The reality is that these people are suffering even as they are still in this country, they are suffering in many ways.

(asylum seeker, Somalia)

This contrasts sharply with newspaper headlines such as '£80m benefits spree for asylum seekers', and the comment that Glasgow's asylum seekers receive 'a whopping £80 MILLION in benefits as they wait to find out if they can stay' (*Scottish Sun*, 11 November 2011; see page 110).

The economic crisis was observed by a number of people to be making representations of the 'burden' of asylum to the country worse. One interviewee for instance said that the:

Economic crisis affect it because people propagandise going on, because asylum seekers and the refugees taking the jobs off [others and what] that mean for the British people.

(refugee worker/Sri Lankan refugee)

One interviewee argued that, with scarce resources, media coverage that talks about asylum costing people money 'can channel negative behaviour' (youth project worker). Another interviewee spoke of someone she knew who is:

very much a local newspaper-reading [person], and local news on the TV ... and she's very much like 'ell ... how can they get a nice house?' ... She thinks it's costing the country money, and when asked why, says 'Well, I read it in the newspaper.'

(youth project worker)

The events of 9/11 were seen as significant in changing coverage. A youth project worker made the point that:

I think there's a lot of confusion between migration, refugees, terrorism.

The 'red tops' were criticised (for instance, by a youth project worker) for using language like 'bogus asylum seeker' and 'illegal asylum seeker' alongside discussion of fear and crime. The press were also seen as particularly focused on stories of criminality: the *Sun* and the *Daily Mail* were frequently identified in this context. One refugee worker argued that:

Particularly with somebody, if there is a hundred thousand of asylum seekers and one asylum seeker committed crime, I mean they will portray that page the big way, so ... that mean the community with all the people all look at this.

(refugee worker/Sri Lankan refugee)

One asylum seeker commented directly on one of the stories examined in our 2006 sample:

a special programme, when people discuss what happens ... it's a scandal about the previous home secretary. He gave ... free foreign criminals something like that and he lost his ... job [small laugh] after that. So from programmes like this one we can usually we can get these words like deportation or criminals or something like that, but usually these words build British people opinion about asylum seeker.

(asylum seeker, Russia)

Another interviewee argued that:

Because when the media portray one asylum seeker about ... one asylum seeker big problem, a murder for instance, so ... the society will compare that news with all asylum seeker.

(refugee worker/Sri Lankan refugee)

He gave the particular example of 'credit card fraud ... it is done by certain people ... always ... the media ... they think all people is doing this crime'. He said the public assume this is all asylum seekers because of the media portrayal 'especially in London, (Glasgow) also, but lot in London'.

Another story which 'stirred hostility' was raised by a different refugee, who said:

a few years ago... there was a story that asylum seekers trying to kill the swans and eating [them]...when people hear this story, you know, they ... react to that ... because they have a certain way of life [that is seen as under attack, and care is important in how stories are presented].

(refugee worker/Congolese refugee)

Another refugee worker also discussed this, commenting that:

'Asylum seekers ate the queen's swans' is much more eye-catching than

'Asylum seekers integrated happily into life in Norwich and created a very wonderful diversity for the very bored people who already lived there'.

(refugee worker)

An asylum seeker recalled that:

Usually it's words about deportation, deportation about crime, but nobody say how many good things, how many asylum seeker can ... integrate (with the) British community.

(asylum seeker, Russia)

It was emphasised by some that the broader picture of geopolitical pressures and trends causing the global refugee situation is largely omitted from the media, leading to a lack of public understanding:

They need actually to say why people are claiming asylum and also ... the origin of the wars. What creates war in the world. ... what creates this situation in first place and then people will understand why people are actually leaving this country.

(refugee worker/Congolese refugee)

One interviewee, a Scottish politician, commented on the need:

To see greater emphasis on our role and responsibility in the world. What we've done over the time and history to make living conditions in certain countries unbearable. How we've affected negatively economies, how we've exploited economies.

(Member of the Scottish Parliament)

As we have indicated, there was some consensus that the media, particularly the press, need to show more of 'the journey' of those claiming asylum:

They won't say why someone is leaving, where they're from, what they've experienced there and what they've come through to get here.

(refugee services manager)

The Refugee Council media officer, Karen Goodwin, has stated that exiled journalists especially need the right to work when they claim asylum, to bring their unique insight into reporting on refugee issues.

She criticised the 'lack of opportunity for refugee journalists' who 'cannot get their foot in the door' (at a public seminar, 11 October 2012). This is another factor in the absence in the media of any meaningful discussion of the problems that face refugees and asylum seekers.

The Asylum Process and Life in the United Kingdom

This neglect of refugee voices means that there is little coverage of the actual experience of the system for claiming asylum and its very negative impacts, for example in abandoning people to destitution. The National Asylum Support Service (NASS) was heavily criticised, along with the lack of coverage of the impact that the organisation can have on the lives of refugees. One person argued that 'they can control and take away and make people destitute' (adult literacy co-ordinator). A refugee worker also observed that coverage did not show:

> The kind of anxiety people live under often for years ... or the fact that even when they get a positive result ... from the Home Office, it's not indefinite leave to remain in most cases, it's another few years and a terrible uncertainty of what's going to happen in the future.
>
> (refugee worker)

Another interviewee recognised this as a serious problem in relation to the coverage of the Coalition cuts to the Home Office:

> Everyone's talking about Home Office cuts, but for instance, take these strikes that might happen tomorrow. It's the Home Office cuts that [mean] 'all these people can come in', it's not the Home Office cuts that mean that 20,000 people are waiting another two years.
>
> (asylum worker)

The media coverage was seen as largely negative, with little sympathy for refugees' lives and problems. One interviewee argued for more coverage of 'unaccompanied minors' and coverage showing 'the lack of support they can have around mental health' (youth project worker). There were examples cited of more positive coverage. For example, one woman described powerful footage of the:

> Reaction to dawn raids and seeing the local population – not just the

refugee population in the area – being totally distraught and outraged and the panic. I also remember scenes from outside the so-called detention centre.

(charity support officer)

A change in recent years to the style of coverage was observed by some:

There's always debates around the numbers of people coming into the country and is Britain being swarmed by people waiting at Calais and such ... but more recently there has been a ... push towards diversifying those forms of representation.

(youth project worker)

This interviewee recalled a TV programme:

For Refugee Week in June ... which can be used in schools, called 'Seeking refuge' ... it's a lot of short clips about different refugees ... which seeks to promote understanding, of the sort of difficulties that people may have been through and it looks at the positive and negative aspects.

(youth project worker)

This was an animated series for children, but was said to have been shown at '4 o'clock on a Saturday morning' so was not as accessible as other media programming. The interviewee argued that coverage of this kind was still a 'drop in the ocean' compared with the negative coverage.

The BBC's *Asylum Night*, aired in 2003, was recalled and received particular criticism from one interviewee:

a really disgusting thing the BBC done about making a decision on somebody's claim, *Asylum Night*, which I think had good intentions ... [it] trivialised the decisions we were having to make towards people's protection.

(medical support worker)

Asylum Night involved a show called 'You the judge' in which viewers were shown four asylum applicants' case histories and asked to decide which of them deserved to stay in the United Kingdom. The public vote on whether individuals should be granted asylum was criticized by our interviewee because 'this isn't a show' and:

If you've disclosed to somebody some of the most painful abuse you've ever experienced and then receive a letter saying we don't believe you, the psychological impact of that is huge.

(medical support worker)

One interviewee said she thought Channel 4 *Dispatches* and BBC *Panorama* 'perceive the reality of being an asylum seeker in the UK' (refugee services manager). Another observed that her local radio:

Always have a number of people in during Refugee Week to talk about their experiences and ... the programmes that we run (on) what diversity is doing for Norwich.

(refugee worker, original emphasis)

The lack of refugee voices in the media was described as being at least in part because of their trauma and their reluctance to share their stories. This interviewee said:

A few of the Congolese refugees who came through Gateway Protection Programme[1].... were happy to tell their stories. Most of the people who I work with who have come through the asylum system ... really don't want to talk about their past.

(refugee worker)

Asylum seekers who come here are often 'in hiding' and are too afraid for themselves and their families at home to talk to the media; this might attract the attention of those they are fleeing from.[2] This is why it is important that refugee rights groups gain access to the media. One refugee worker argued that their advocacy in the media is especially important:

When it come to raising awareness about how officials here in the UK, in European countries treat people claiming asylum. When it is done properly, then we have changes in law.

(Congolese refugee/refugee worker)

---

1 The Gateway Protection Programme is a resettlement programme run by the UNHCR, under which the UK government agrees to accept up to 750 refugees per year. It gives 'some of the worlds' most vulnerable refugees' a safe route to refuge in the 30 participating countries, and operates separately from the normal asylum route (see www.refugee-action.org.uk/ourwork/projects/Gateway.aspx).

2 Fictional representations were seen as important. For example one refugee worker said BBC 'Radio 4 plays are great' (refugee services manager).

He argued such groups' inclusion in the media was crucial in communicating asylum seekers' rights over the issue of 'illegal entry' – an area in which confusion exists both in the media representation (as many of our examples have shown) and in public awareness. He said:

> You think about someone who has fled his country arriving in the UK with false document and get arrested, put in jail. So that person has already experienced trauma just for leaving his family, leaving everything and arriving, seeking protection but rather than protection what [do] they get? They get prison sentence.
>
> (Congolese refugee/refugee worker)

This man reported having seen this scenario many times lead to the person's deportation back to the place they fled from or their suicide.

An asylum seeker argued that the media do not investigate suicides in detention centres, or the tragedy when refugees are deported as 'failed' asylum seekers:

> Even some people they take to their country they die…. They just take them and really leave them there. You know somebody that flee, there, how many of them is safe? How many of them is alive? They don't care if people die here, commit suicide here, they just go and bury the person, nobody will talk, nobody will, you know, and television doesn't reveal all these things.
>
> (asylum seeker, Somalia)

The hostile coverage was attacked for not giving an accurate account and ignoring the problems that asylum seekers face: 'they don't show how asylum seekers living, the state they are in the community' or how 'isolated' they are (asylum seeker, Somalia). One asylum seeker pointed out that:

> Any journalist can come to [an asylum seeker's] house and describe how they live, how these people now love this country, how these people want to, to do this country better … they can describe … how these people usually in the evening they go, … to sleep and they have to wake up maybe around 4 or 5 am because … they stay in dangerous … to be deported arrested in early morning, it's terrible. I think it's good idea to spend one night in their flat and after show us from … in TV programme … about true life asylum seeker in Scotland for example.
>
> (asylum seeker, Russia)

The media also were said not to show what were described as the negative and antagonistic attitudes of some public officials:

> The way they be controlling you in the immigration office, they will be swearing at you. Even officers swearing at you, 'Fuck, fuck, fuck, fuck', you know, swearing at you or everything you are doing. You will go there and sometimes they will keep you ... [you] know, for two, three hours you know, keep you for two, three hours. Signing [as present] with the children ... even if you are blind, even if you are lame.
>
> (asylum seeker, Somalia)

When coverage focuses on the 'negative impacts' of asylum seekers coming to the United Kingdom, refugees become fearful of hostility: 'people are just scared' by the coverage and the impact it will have (refugee worker/Congolese refugee). This perception of public opinion was seen to increase feelings of intimidation in the asylum claim interview and in their interactions with immigration officials.

The media coverage in conjunction with the Home Office approach was also seen as a factor contributing to illegal working. Refugees go 'underground' through fear, and those who do this are then seen as 'illegal' economic migrants. This interviewee observed that the 'attitude of the Home Office is scaremongering' and this has repercussions for refugees. When the media shows the authorities 'detaining one person', then:

> Ten person will be disappear from the system ... A lot of people they are scared to go to Home Office so they will disappear. They will go to any employer, and one pound two pound they will give them.
>
> (refugee worker/Sri Lankan refugee)

He stressed that he knew genuine refugees were doing this, and his wife backed this up:

> The people are scared. The real asylum seekers don't come forward because if they get into the system they end up in a detention [centre] and they end up deported .... Underground is better than get deported and get killed.
>
> (refugee, Sri Lanka)

This does raise the question of what is the point of such government actions other than as media-driven public relations, especially if the actions are counterproductive and simply increase the pressure on already vulnerable communities.

Community Impacts

The influence of media coverage on public understanding was also commented on, and again parallels the findings of our focus groups:

> They never tell the public that asylum seeker not allowed to work and people they will think asylum seeker are just lazy people who can't do anything, who just came to put more expenses on the government and taxpayer who have to pay all that and make the public hate asylum seeker and refugee.
>
> (asylum seeker, Rwanda)

The media were seen as justifying and reinforcing negative attitudes and behaviour:

> It highlights something they wouldn't previously [have] thought of, you look at the recession and people start to go, all these people are coming into our country and we haven't got enough money as it is.
>
> (youth project worker)

The perception that the mode of entry makes someone an 'illegal immigrant' was said by one refugee worker to have been taken on by a refugee she worked with:

> One very well-informed Iraqi woman who'd come through the Gateway ... Protection Programme was in an English class with several asylum seekers ... and she said that she had come to this country legally because she had come through the Gateway Protection Programme but asylum seekers came illegally. And I said no, no ... it's just as legal to come as an asylum seeker, but she felt that ... because she had been selected that made her more legal and the others less legal.
>
> (refugee worker)

Only a small number enter the United Kingdom through Gateway Protection. The same interviewee (a refugee worker from Norwich) gave another example of an elderly woman whose husband was a Polish refugee from Auschwitz. The refugee worker was talking about her work with refugees, and the woman asked, 'Are any of them genuine?' She believed that contemporary asylum seekers are not genuine refugees because of what she had seen in the media, despite having a personal connection to someone who had sought refuge.

The conflation of asylum with wider immigration debates has also impacted on larger communities of economic migrants in Britain. One interviewee noted that:

> Everybody's lumped together, so ... we've run international friendship groups where we've had several women who are the wives of foreign students or ... men working in international companies ... who are living here and they're very much seen as, you know, asylum seekers and refugees who are scrounging off the state.
>
> (refugee worker)

The negative media coverage focusing on 'illegality' and a 'burden' was said to lead to misperceptions about asylum seekers' entitlements:

> People believe that every asylum seeker is given a mobile phone and has unlimited access ... to legal aid and ... given ... council houses ahead of local families. They don't believe that asylum seekers aren't anywhere in the local housing.
>
> (refugee worker)

This was seen as emphasising divisions in society by some interviewees, as in this comment:

> The media portray[al] of people claiming asylum as coming in Britain to take over the jobs ... this is a negative impact that is the media is trying to separate the population.
>
> (refugee worker/Congolese refugee)

The failure to explain that asylum seekers have a forced dependence on the state and charity was also said to affect future opportunities:

> I am around 48 years old and now I don't have [the] last eleven years. When I go to a job and they ask what eleven years you done? I [was] an asylum seeker. No chance, in this current situation, no chance. No getting a job.
>
> (refugee worker/Sri Lankan refugee)

Media coverage was also identified as a primary cause of the violence and verbal abuse directed at asylum seekers:

> I have the experience myself. Once the TV showed asylum seekers given money. They are eating the tax of people working here. Once you go outside people are shouting at you, 'You are taking my money. Go away [to] your country, go away to the jungle.' We didn't understand why the media are doing this to us.
>
> (asylum seeker, Sudan)

Media coverage was also linked to the way children were treated by their peers. An asylum seeker said:

> Children in school started telling our asylum seeker children, 'I saw you on the TV, you are not normal', and they make our children not feel they belong here because they are different.
>
> (asylum seeker, Sudan)

One youth worker commented that young asylum seekers:

> Don't want to be labelled an asylum seeker or a refugee ... if they go to college and some of them are very nervous about talking about their past to people because of the opinion that they might then have of them.
>
> (youth project worker)

One asylum seeker told of verbal abuse she had received on the bus as a result of a person's perception of asylum:

> I was sitting on the bus seat for the older people so I stood up and I wanted him to sit but he swore and he did [not] sit. He refused to sit in there, he was an old man but he swore and complained about asylum seekers all the way until he got off the bus. ... All these people taking, starting from his seat, who are taking all these things. He was so angry. Oh I just looked at him; I just looked at him because I knew he doesn't know anything.
>
> (asylum seeker, Uganda)

Community impacts extended beyond verbal abuse, and another asylum seeker expressed suicidal feelings resulting from his treatment. He described abuse and fear:

People sometimes you know, some of the places, even where I'm staying itself they murdered [an] illegal immigrant. They murdered him, an asylum seeker, called him illegal immigrant, you know. Because they are taking refuge, they are taking free house, free water, free money, free oh, you know that is it. It's always what they, the way they present it make people, raise people's anger over illegal ... over asylum seekers or illegal immigrants as they call them. It makes them, it makes them, it raise their anger. Well, that's why they're always fighting. That's why they always, even where I was in Sunderland they murdered asylum, two asylum seekers, the same flat where they kept me when I seek asylum you know. Even in Glasgow here, even in Glasgow they murdered one Chinese guy. So these are the things that make people feel angry about them, and when they see them. Even myself, I don't walk in the night, sometimes if I go I be hiding because they be swearing on you, swearing on me because of all these things they hear on the news, saying we are taking their house, we are taking their money, we are taking their benefit. So they will be swearing every time, you know.

(asylum seeker, Somalia)

The voucher support system was criticised for making it easy to identify asylum seekers and leaving them vulnerable to this abuse:

If you go in the shop you know, everybody will know that you are asylum seeker or illegal immigrant. Sometimes people will start swearing at you in the shop there because they know the voucher is for illegal immigrant.

(asylum seeker, Somalia)

The coverage of deportations and the accusations of 'illegality' and fraud in the media were said to affect the mental health of refugees and asylum seekers, particularly when the media show them:

Arresting people like, paper and television tell the stories like ... detaining asylum seekers and big propaganda like we arrested three people, two people, ... and it affects ... real asylum seekers. ... Because they are scared. And a lot [of] the problem [is] because a lot of asylum seekers don't understand English. So whatever they are seeing on television it doing a negative effect on them. And a pressure on them, and a lot of them, their mental health is affected.

(refugee, Sri Lanka)

Another refugee commented that:

There about ten, eleven people in my organisation they are mentally affected. They got papers, everything, but scared. Still the problem going on. They just spending huge money on them. Because it is created by the Home Office. ... It's waiting maybe to get deported, ... what happen with this next knock from Home Office ... So it's everyday possibility.

(refugee worker/Sri Lankan refugee)

Our interviewee then described someone he worked with who had been in Glasgow for nine years. He had been granted asylum:

But somebody knocking on the door, he very scared. Still he scared. ... So he's under care of the ... psychiatric doctors and also, he's getting lot of money from the disability allowance or something, but OK ... but why are you creating these people that way? You create the situation and then you spending money on them after.

(refugee worker/Sri Lankan refugee)

Another asylum seeker confirmed the impacts that negative coverage, which does not cover the day-to-day realities of seeking asylum, has on the mental health of vulnerable people:

Even most of the people themselves anti-depression because of the way they been treated, anti-depression it very hard before you find any asylum, any asylum seeker that is not in anti-depression. A lot of people kill themselves even when I'm in detention you know so that is it. They don't tell people the reality, they don't tell them how really how these people are living you know.

(asylum seeker, Somalia)

Some interviewees spoke of the pressures in their local areas and of how refugees were targeted for abuse and attacks. One who was employed in an asylum support team described how new arrivals lived:

People were living in fear, many people had been burgled or targeted for burglaries or had faced verbal and physical abuse, when they left their home, particularly at the start, of when they first came to Glasgow. There was one woman who lived in a flat in Govan and she had a lot of torment by locals when she moved into a block of flats.

(asylum support worker)

This interviewee also commented on the reasons that had underpinned the dispersal policy and how the policy was perceived by local residents:

> The reason why they were put in Glasgow was because of the number of high-rise flats that were lying empty so the councils thought as they had these flats lying empty, we'll accommodate them and get money. They could accommodate people all over the empty flats in Glasgow but the locals did not want this.
>
> (asylum support worker)

The reality of what was offered was very different from popular perception:

> The reality was the asylum seekers got poor-quality housing, housing that was full of dampness that was not looked after very well, but the council got everybody in and made money out of it by getting rent for them. But the local people actually were so against it, and it was such a culture shock for them to see people from different communities wearing different kinds of clothes, living on their doorstep as their neighbours, they found that really difficult. I know this as I had loads of folk speaking to me in high-rise flats.
>
> (asylum support worker)

The crucial point is made here that the negative media coverage of asylum and refugees legitimised the attacks on the new arrivals:

> The media was reporting on what was happening at the time about this dispersal scheme going on at the time and can imagine what the people take from that as well, it gives people, it sanitises their beliefs to say it's OK to single out people.
>
> (asylum support worker)

Another argued that coverage can be important in forming opinions when people:

> Don't know about us, they don't know about problems. They just think you are coming just to take money, eat and drink and stay home and have all the things free. That's not true.
>
> (asylum seeker, Sudan)

This interviewee also gave the example of a candlelight vigil in

Glasgow to try to stop a deportation, suggesting that informed understanding leads to empathy:

> The Scottish people when they are going to work they just asking us, 'Why you are standing like this?' and we tell them this is happening. Most of them they come and join us there. The second day they came because before they don't know why these people are standing outside.
>
> (asylum seeker, Sudan)

While some people we interviewed felt that 'people who aren't interested in asylum issues don't watch those programmes' (refugee worker), when the media did raise an issue, supportive coverage that examined the problems facing asylum seekers was often seen as having a great positive impact on society and public understanding. One interviewee stated that when the media take on an issue such as in the case of children being held in detention centres, 'people then will take over' (and the issue will gain momentum). They understand and 'try to see what contribution they can make', but if the media do not cover such issues, the public remain unaware (refugee worker/ Congolese refugee). This man argued that positive coverage leads to a 'change in the way [immigration officials] treat people', and pointed to the example of children in detention, a practice which he argued was halted by a media campaign.

These interviews reinforce many of the key issues about media coverage that have been raised elsewhere in the study. They highlight the absence of the voices of refugees and their representatives, and the negative and distorted nature of much reporting. But they also show the impact of media coverage, and media distortions, on the lives of very vulnerable people. This combination of media attacks and punitive government policy fuels the stigmatisation of refugees and their social isolation, as well as actually intensifying many of the problems that the policies are allegedly addressing.

Conclusion

There are five key issues that we identify in this study. The first is the persistent and overwhelmingly hostile coverage of refugees and asylum in much of the national media. The second is the confusion in news accounts between refugees, asylum seekers and other migrants. The third is the relative absence of the voices of refugees or those who represent them, as any form of balance to the inaccurate and partial reporting. Fourth are the consequences, of this coverage and the policies which it encourages, for the stability of existing communities in the United Kingdom. Finally there are consequences for the refugees themselves, particularly the effect of the media in further isolating and stigmatizing them.

As we have argued, in a society which is already heavily stratified between rich and poor, the arrival of new groups whether they are poor economic migrants or destitute refugees can put pressure on the poorest areas of that society as they struggle for already scarce resources in health, housing and education. The media can respond in different ways to this. It could focus on the plight of the new arrivals and pressure policy makers to respond to the needs of refugees or other groups by directing appropriate resources and reducing the stress in local areas. It could also point to the role of the West in contributing both to the economic problems of the developing world and to some of the conflicts that have produced large-scale population movements. Or it could exploit the potential tensions created by these movements for its own commercial advantage (in attempts to increase market share of readers, listeners or viewers). Some politicians effectively do the same thing to generate popular support for right-wing, populist and nationalist policies. Such rhetoric also functions to reduce public discussion of the impact of other factors such as the financial and economic crisis, the recession and the inadequacy of political responses to these. In this sense, asylum seekers may join a long list of convenient scapegoats including the unemployed, those claiming benefits and those registered as disabled. It is clear from our analysis of press and television content which direction the bulk of the media took in relation to their presentation of asylum and refugees. Such media accounts have a crucial impact in legitimising the hostility toward and bullying of the new arrivals.

One of our interviewees who worked on a large council estate described how a culture of belief and false generalisations without evidence becomes pervasive in everyday conversation:

> People say things to me like 'These people are getting loads of benefits', and I ask how many people they actually know that have actually got these things, give me some evidence. Most say they don't know anybody so I ask where their opinion comes from. Can you give me an example of who has a free home or better home than you? If you're telling me this is true, where is the evidence? There is none, it's just that people are getting these opinions through the media, people then gossip and it is coming from negative articles in the media. If one article discusses that Afghani family, then it will become an issue and all Afghani families will be assumed to be doing the same.
>
> (Group 1, British Asian male)

We have pointed to the intense stress that this climate of hostility imposes on individuals and communities. At its height the press hysteria coincided with actual physical attacks on asylum seekers. One television journalist told us that he believed that the press coverage was so appalling that in his view, some papers should have been prosecuted for incitement to violence. Another journalist from a major broadsheet used a phrase which was in our minds as we wrote this work. He spoke of an editor sending a young reporter to 'go and monster an asylum seeker'. So the decision is open and clear to the point that the word 'monster' is used, as in 'make a monster of a person'. In the introduction to the third edition of Stanley Cohen's classic work *Folk Devils and Moral Panics* (2011), the author points to asylum seekers as new 'folk devils', listing several examples of hostile coverage. While acknowledging that causal links are 'hard to prove', he states that:

> In three days in August 2001 a Kurdish asylum seeker was stabbed to death on a Glasgow housing estate and two other Kurds attacked. The UNHCR issued a statement saying that this was predictable 'given the climate of vilification of asylum seekers that has taken hold of the UK

in recent years.' This branding has become so successful that 'asylum seeker' and 'refugee' have become terms of abuse in school playgrounds.

(Cohen, 2011: XXV)

Some of our interviewees pointed to specific newspapers or television programmes associated with very negative coverage. As we saw above, the programme *UK Border Force* was referred to by a participant as offering a simple good and bad vision of the world, with nothing heard from people seeking asylum. In 2008 it was reported that the Home Office had paid £400,000 to an independent production company to help fund the series for Sky Television. The money had then been later handed back by Sky 'in an effort to escape the controversy building around the government's investment in advertising-funded programming' (Davidson, 2008). However, the programme was 'overseen by the Central Office of Information' at the Border Agency, and this £400,000 was 'only one part of a wider £2 million that had been spent by the government on sponsoring other 'documentaries', according to the Institute of Race Relations (Burnett, 2009).

This is an interesting example of the interaction between government and media. We have seen in the content analysis in earlier chapters how journalists focus on alleged problems and question politicians on what they have done to resolve them. On *Channel Four News* for example, the newscaster asks a government minister, 'How many employers have you prosecuted in the last year for employing illegal immigrants? ... You know we could go to endless places, anywhere in Britain' (17 May 2006). Governments respond to such questions by highlighting their own actions. In the above case, they actually put money back into the media to advertise their own activities, which were addressing the climate of fear which had itself been fanned by the media. If paying for advertising proves difficult, governments can supply other public relations material and use their normal techniques of information management to highlight their policy response to the alleged problem. The police, or immigration officials mount high-profile raids seeking 'illegal migrants' and 'failed asylum seekers' and these can be filmed and provide material for more media coverage. This creates a perfect circle of media coverage, government and 'official' action.

These images of a 'threat' being dealt with stand in sharp contrast to the actual conditions to which near-destitute and excluded people are reduced by the policies directed at them. The 'policy initiatives' are legitimised by much of the media coverage, but as we have seen, very little of this deals with their human consequences. This is an issue raised by Zoe Williams in the *Guardian*, in which she described the Kafkaesque life imposed on people who are on Section 4 asylum support. She described the Azure card, which means that:

> benefits, such as they are, come in vouchers rather than cash, so you can't get a bus or make a phone call, can't post a letter or buy a pint of milk from your corner shop. You have to be housed three miles from a shop that takes your Azure card; that can mean a six-mile walk every time you want to buy something.
>
> (Williams, 2013)

She described the findings of a parliamentary enquiry, chaired by Sarah Teather (2013), and noted how people are rendered homeless without support:

> A family slept for months on the floor of a mosque. A woman had twins prematurely, lost one and had to walk to and from the hospital to keep appointments for the other, carrying the baby and an oxygen cylinder. A woman gave birth while her benefits were delayed, and had to carry her newborn home in her arms, because she didn't have [a] buggy or any money for a bus.
>
> (Williams, 2013)

And she asks what is the purpose of treating people in this way. Is it vindictive or just political point scoring?

> If it doesn't save money, the purpose is either vindictive – a genuine malice borne by the home secretary towards foreigners in need – or it's political, Theresa May backing up her tough, tough talk about how human rights are rubbish because someone she heard about at the Ukip Conference of Made Up Case Studies couldn't be deported because he had a cat.
>
> (Williams 2013)

There are no easy recommendations to be made here. When large sections of the media are in collusion with governments who have popular support for policies that bully and stigmatise refugees, then it is a difficult road. But we can campaign for more accurate reporting, and an end to stigmatizing and false descriptions such as 'illegals' or terms such as 'parasites' and 'scroungers'. We can demand that the television news services fulfil their obligations in relation to balance by allowing refugees and asylum seekers to tell their own stories. The Leveson Inquiry into the conduct of the press offers a glimmer of hope. It reported on evidence from a variety of groups recognizing the lack of truth in stories and the consistently distorted nature of coverage:

> 8.46 The Joint Council on the Welfare of Immigrants, the Migrant and Refugee Communities Forum, and the Federation of Poles in Great Britain gave evidence that supported and complemented each other. Together, their evidence suggested that the approach of parts of the press to migrants and asylum seekers was one of advocacy rather than reporting: some newspapers expressed a consistently clear view on the harm caused by migrants and/or asylum seekers (often conflating the two) and ensured that any coverage of the issue fit within that narrative.
> (Leveson, 2012)

In the redress of such issues, press regulation might help. But the problem is deeper in that there is a complex interaction between media accounts, government actions and public attitudes. We have shown how media coverage can highlight and stimulate potential tensions and fears by stigmatising refugees and asylum seekers. This legitimises negative official and public responses. Communities are destabilised and the physical and mental health of those seeking refuge is compromised. The policy is counterproductive, as a humane approach to the vulnerable is replaced by punitive measures encouraged by media accounts that are hysterical in tone, partial and inaccurate.

We must go beyond simply criticizing such coverage and argue for a humane and rational approach to the issue of refuge and asylum, and do so in public spaces through the lobbying of political parties, and support for existing groups that attempt to help and protect refugees, using whatever access to new and old media is possible. We can demand accuracy and balance in media reporting, but also humanity in public life and political policy. and the right of the stigmatized and excluded to be heard.

APPENDIX ONE

Guide to the Asylum Process

The information below draws upon the Refugee Council publication *Brief Guide to Asylum* (2013).

Who seeks asylum

There were 19,865 applications for asylum in the United Kingdom in 2011. In 2012, during the first nine months there were 15,569 applications. The top ten countries of origin of 'asylum seekers' are Pakistan, Iran, Sri Lanka, India, Bangladesh, Afghanistan, Syria, Nigeria, Albania and Eritrea. In 2011 and 2012 there was an increase in applicant numbers from Libya and Syria (Refugee Council, 2013).

The Application Process and Detained Fast Track (DFT)

Applications for asylum must be made to an immigration officer upon arrival at a port of entry into the United Kingdom or at the Asylum Screening Unit in Croydon. Some 'asylum seekers' are detained in a detention/removal centre at the point when they make the application, and are put into the detained fast track (DFT). Cases taken through DFT have a very high refusal rate. In 2011 of 2,118 cases in the DFT only 66 (3 per cent) were granted refugee status, and seven were granted humanitarian protection or discretionary leave to remain. Just 5 per cent of appeals were successful. There has been considerable criticism of the DFT, including by the independent chief inspector of the UK Border Agency (UKBA).

Asylum applicants not on the DFT have to attend a screening

interview soon after their initial application. This interview collects information such as identity, country of origin, when and how the person arrived in the United Kingdom, and what documents they have, such as a passport or other identity papers. The asylum seeker is fingerprinted and a photo is taken which is put on the application registration card (ARC) which is issued to them. The card may be the only legal identification which an asylum seeker possesses. It has printed on the front of it NO PERMISSION TO WORK.

A second, more detailed substantive interview then takes place. The information from the first interview is double checked to ensure a consistent account is given. The asylum seeker also has to provide evidence to back up their asylum claim and show that they are in need of protection and cannot safely be returned to their country of origin.

While the application is under consideration the asylum seeker is required to report within consistent time frames (such as daily, weekly or monthly) to one of the 14 UKBA reporting centres or a police station. The person may be expected to travel within a 25-mile radius or up to 90 minutes. They are expected to produce their ARC when they report. Reporting is also referred to as 'signing'. Failure to report can lead to detention and the withdrawal of asylum support (NASS) (Refugee Council, 2013).

The Decision on the Application

A caseworker decides whether the applicant qualifies for recognition as a refugee under the terms of the 1951 UN Convention Relating to the Status of Refugees. According to the Convention a person who has reason to fear persecution in their country because of their race, religion, nationality, membership of a particular social group or political opinion, should be recognised as a refugee.

Applicants who are granted refugee status by UKBA are given leave to remain in the United Kingdom for five years. They are free to work, and are eligible for mainstream benefits. If they have a spouse and children outside the United Kingdom these can apply to join the refugee in the United Kingdom. After five years they can apply for indefinite leave to remain.

Some people who are not granted refugee status are given permission to remain. A number are granted humanitarian protection, which means that UKBA does not believe their case justifies refugee status, but does accept that the person cannot safely be returned to their own country. Humanitarian protection is normally for five years. Others are granted discretionary leave to remain for a time-limited period, after which they may be able to apply to extend their leave. Many of these cases involve unaccompanied children seeking asylum. If asylum is refused they are granted discretionary leave to remain to reflect the government's position that lone children will not be returned unless there are adequate conditions for them to be looked after in the country of return. The child has to make another application to request leave for a further period (Refugee Council, 2013).

How Many People are Granted Refugee Status

In recent years the percentage of applicants granted refugee status has varied from 17 to 25 per cent. The refusal rate has varied from 64 to 74 per cent. The remainder have been granted humanitarian protection or discretionary leave. Many groups including the UNHCR, Amnesty International, the Home Affairs and Constitutional Committees, the Lords EU Committee and the National Audit Office have expressed concern about the quality of Home Office decision making (Refugee Council, 2013).

Appeals Against Refusal

An asylum seeker whose claim is refused generally has a right of appeal against the decision. They are expected to lodge their appeal within ten days of receiving the decision. They must put forward at the same time any other arguments, such as a case based on human rights, why they should be allowed to remain in the United Kingdom. The appeal decision is made by an immigration judge at a tribunal hearing. The Asylum and Immigration (Treatment of Claimants) Act 2004 created a new system of appeals which allows for only one appeal. Previously people could lodge a second appeal in another court if their first appeal was rejected. If the second appeal was rejected then in exceptional circumstances they could apply for their case to be heard in the High Court. The proportion of appeals allowed has been in the range 25–30 per cent in recent years, so a significant number of initial decisions are found to be wrong by the tribunal (Refugee Council, 2013).

Removal of People Whose Claim is Refused

People who have been refused, and have lost their appeal, are expected to return to their country of origin. Some will return on a voluntary basis, otherwise UKBA will enforce removal from the United Kingdom. The exceptions are usually people whom UKBA accepts cannot safely be returned. They may be allowed to remain in the United Kingdom until conditions in their country of origin permit safe return. In 2011 just over 7,500 refused asylum seekers and dependants were forcibly removed from the United Kingdom, and around 2,500 of these were voluntary departures. UKBA employs private security firms to carry out forced removals/deportations. Injuries and deaths have been sustained by those subject to forced removals. Three hundred allegations were made of assault between 2004 and 2008. Two people died of asphyxiation and suffocation during a forced removal (Refugee Council, 2013).

Social Support and Accommodation for Asylum Seekers

The Immigration and Asylum Act 1999 removed asylum seekers' entitlement to welfare, housing benefits or support from local authorities. They were made subject to an entirely separate support regime, administered directly by the Home Office. A new division within the Home Office, the National Asylum Support Service (NASS), was established. The responsibility for social support shifted entirely from the former Department of Social Security and local authorities to the Home Office. Asylum seekers are not allowed to claim mainstream benefits. They are not allowed to work, unless their application is still undetermined after a year, in which case they can apply for permission to work, but this applies to very few people.

To qualify for support from UKBA the asylum seeker has to show that they are over 18, have applied for asylum upon arrival in the United Kingdom, and are unable to support themselves. 'Asylum' seekers applying to UKBA for support can apply for accommodation and cash. If UKBA accept an application for accommodation and cash the asylum seeker is offered accommodation on a no-choice basis outside London and the South East. Some people are required to share accommodation with other people seeking asylum. They are subject to being moved to different accommodation anywhere in the United Kingdom at any time, and are moved regularly. Currently UKBA has contracts with a number of private companies to provide accommodation in different parts of the country.

Examples of the level of cash support provided are £72.52 per week for a couple, £43.94 for a lone parent and £42.62 for a single person over 25. For comparison for people claiming a mainstream benefit (income support) the levels are £111.45 for a couple both over 18, and £71.00 for a lone parent or a single person over 25. The level of cash support has not increased since April 2011 (Refugee Council, 2013).

Support, Accommodation, Azure Cards and Destitution for Refused Asylum Seekers

Asylum seekers with children under the age of 18 who have been refused refugee status are entitled to receive NASS support until they leave, or are removed from, the United Kingdom. Single people are only entitled to 'Section 4' support, and only when they meet one of a number of tightly defined conditions. These include demonstrating willingness to leave the United Kingdom, having a medical reason not to travel, or being unable to travel because there is no safe route of return. The person must be destitute or about to become so.

If UKBA agree to Section 4 support it may provide basic self-catering accommodation and support to the value of £35.39 per week. The support is not in cash, but is loaded onto the Azure support card, which entails restricted use for food and toiletries in a number of shops such as Asda and Tesco. Figures available in September 2012 show just over 2,500 people were in receipt of Section 4 support. If an applications for Section 4 support is refused then they are left destitute. Forty-eight per cent of visits to refugee charities are from destitute people, many of whom have been in that situation for longer than six months (Refugee Council, 2013).

Detention

Another point in the asylum process at which detention occurs is at its end, when refused asylum seekers are liable for detention prior to forced removal from the United Kingdom. Of 12,800 asylum detainees in 2011 just under half were forcibly removed from the United Kingdom on leaving detention, and the remainder were released, bailed, granted temporary admission, or granted leave to remain. There is a high rate of suicides and self-harm incidents in detention/removal centres. In the last ten years there have been over 20 suicides in detention. There was a 25 per cent increase in self-harming between 2008 and 2009, with 215 incidents of self-harm requiring medical treatment in 2009, compared with 179 incidents in 2008 (Refugee Council, 2013).

Further information and links

Refugee Council policy and statistics briefings:
    www.refugeecouncil.org.uk/policy/briefings
    www.refugeecouncil.org.uk/practice/basics/truth.htm
Home Office research and detailed statistics:
    www.homeoffice.gov.uk/publications/science-research-statistics/
research-statistics/immigration-asylum-research/
UKBA, The asylum process and asylum support:
    www.ukba.homeoffice.gov.uk/asylum/
UKBA: Policy and law, staff guidance and instructions, and immigration rules:
    www.ukba.homeoffice.gov.uk/policyandlaw/
Independent Chief Inspector of Borders and Immigration:
    http://icinspector.independent.gov.uk/
HM Inspector of Prisons reports on immigration removal centres:
    www.justice.gov.uk/publications/inspectorate-reports/
hmi-prisons

APPENDIX TWO

Interviewees

Refugee Workers

1 Community development officer
2 Community development officer
3 Media development officer
4 Adult literacy coordinator
5 Youth project coordinator
6 Lecturer
7 Medical support manager
8 Charity support officer
9 Social worker
10 Literacy tutor
11 Literacy tutor
12 Youth project worker 1
13 Youth project worker 2
14 Member of the Scottish Parliament (MSP)
15 Glasgow city councillor
16 Refugee worker
17 Refugee services manager
18 Refugee worker and Congolese refugee
19 Refugee worker and Sri Lankan refugee
20 Asylum worker.

Refugees and Asylum Seekers

1 Female, Sri Lankan refugee
2 Male, Somalia, seeking asylum for five years
3 Male, Russia, seeking asylum for six years
4 Male, Pakistan, seeking asylum

5 Female, Uganda, seeking asylum

6 Female, Nigerian, seeking asylum for six years

7 Female, Sudan, seeking asylum for four years

8 Female, Lebanon, seeking asylum

9 Female, Rwanda, seeking asylum for five years

10 Male, Sri Lanka, refugee status

11 Male, Afghanistan, refugee status

12 Male, Zimbabwe, seeking asylum

13 Male, Georgia/ Abkhazia, seeking asylum for nine years

14 Male, Sudan, seeking asylum

15 Female, Azerbaijan, seeking asylum for five years

16 Male, Iraq, seeking asylum for six years.

References

Alia, V. and Bull, S. (2005) *Media and Ethnic Minorities*, Edinburgh: Edinburgh University Press.

Article 19 (2003) 'What's the story? Media representation of refugees and asylum seekers in the UK'. Available from: www.article19.org/data/files/pdfs/publications/refugees-what-s-the-story-.pdf

Bardhan, Pranab (1990) 'Symposium on the state and economic development', *Journal of Economic Perspectives*, vol. 4, no. 3.

BBC (2011) 'Breaking into Britain', *Panorama*, online, 16 June.

BBC News (2000a) 'Asylum camp plan attacked', BBC Online, 18 April. Available from: http://news.bbc.co.uk/1/hi/uk_politics/718111.stm

BBC News (2000b) 'Illegal immigrants: UK overview', BBC Online, 27 June. Available from: http://news.bbc.co.uk/1/hi/world/europe/797491.stm

BBC News (2005) 'Howard unveils Tory asylum plans', BBC Online, 24 January. Available from: http://news.bbc.co.uk/1/hi/uk_politics/4200761.stm

BBC News (2006a) 'Tory pledge on Human Rights Act', BBC Online, 12 May. Available from: http://news.bbc.co.uk/1/hi/uk_politics/4765861.stm

BBC News (2006b) 'Blair sparks new deportation row', BBC Online, 17 May. Available from: http://news.bbc.co.uk/2/hi/uk_news/politics/4988756.stm (accessed April 22, 2013).

BBC News (2006c) 'Immigration system unfit – Reid', BBC Online, 23 May. Available from: http://news.bbc.co.uk/1/hi/uk_politics/5007148.stm

BBC News (2009a) 'Human Rights Act defended by DPP', BBC Online, 21 October. Available from: http://news.bbc.co.uk/1/hi/uk/8318960.stm

BBC News (2009b) 'Q and A: the banana wars', BBC Online, 15 December. Available from: http://news.bbc.co.uk/1/hi/business/8390099.stm

Bennett, Natalie (2007) 'Seek and ye shall not find', *Guardian*, 31 May. Available from: www.guardian.co.uk/commentisfree/2007/may/31/seekandyeshallnotfind

Blair, Tony (2004) 'Full text of Blair's speech'. BBC Online, 28 September. Available from: http://news.bbc.co.uk/1/hi/uk_politics/3697434.stm

Blinder, S. (2011) 'Migration to the UK: asylum', Oxford Migration Observatory, 5 December. Available from: http://migrationobservatory.ox.ac.uk/briefings/migration-uk-asylum

Blood Coltan (2008) documentary film.

Blunkett, D. (2003) 'Fortress Britain', *Evening Standard*, 10 January. Available from: www.standard.co.uk/news/fortress-britain-6351118.html

Briant, E., Watson, N. and Philo, G. (2011) 'Bad news for disabled people', Inclusion London. Available from: www.inclusionlondon.co.uk/domains/ inclusionlondon.co.uk/local/media/downloads/bad_news_for_disabled_ people_pdf.pdf

Briggs, B. (2012) 'Failed asylum seekers in Scotland living below UN global poverty threshold', Guardian Online, 1 October. Available from: www. guardian.co.uk/uk/2012/oct/01/failed-asylum-seekers-scotland-poverty

Brogan, B. (2005) 'It's time to celebrate the Empire, says Brown', *Daily Mail*, 15 January. Available from: www.dailymail.co.uk/news/article-334208/ Its-time-celebrate-Empire-says-Brown.html

Buchanan, S., Grillo, B. and Threadgold, T. (2003) *What's the Story: Sangatte; a case study of media coverage of asylum and refugee issues*, London: Article 19.

Burnett, J (2009) 'PR and the selling of border controls', Institute for Race Relations, 21 May. Available from: www.irr.org.uk/news/ pr-and-the-selling-of-border-controls/

Campbell, Duncan (2006) 'Civil wars create new crisis despite number of refugees falling to lowest level for 25 years', *Guardian*, 16 April. Available from: www.guardian.co.uk/society/2006/apr/19/internationalaidand development.immigrationasylumandrefugees

Casciani, D. (2004) 'Media linked to asylum violence', BBC News, 14 July. Available from: http://news.bbc.co.uk/1/hi/uk/3890963.stm

Castles, S. and Kossack, G. (1973) *Immigrant Workers and Class Structures in Western Europe*, Oxford: Oxford University Press.

Castles, Stephen, Schierup, Carl-Ulrik and Hansen, Peo (2006) *Migration, Citizenship, and the European Welfare State: A European dilemma*, Oxford: Oxford University Press.

Chartered Institute of Housing (CIH) (2008) *Allocations of Social Housing to Recent Migrants: Report for the Local Government Association*, Coventry: CIH.

Chu, B. and Grice, A. (2012) 'Bring in migrants to cut billions from deficit, says Osborne's watchdog', *Independent*, 13 July. Available from: www. independent.co.uk/news/uk/politics/bring-in-migrants-to-cut-billions- from-deficit-says-osbornes-watchdog-7939667.html

Clarke, C. (2006) *Letter from the Home Secretary to the Chairman of the Committee on Public Accounts*, 25 April. Available from: www.publications. parliament.uk/pa/cm200506/cmselect/cmpubacc/1079/6042612.htm

Clements, L. (2007) 'Asylum in crisis, an assessment of UK asylum law and policy since 2002: fear of terrorism or economic efficiency?' Web Journal of Current Legal Issues. Available from: http://webjcli.ncl.ac.uk/2007/ issue3/clements3.html#_Toc170621773

Cohen, S. (2011) *Folk Devils and Moral Panics*, London: Taylor & Francis.

Coussey, M. (2005) *Independent Race Monitor Annual Report 2004–2005*, London: HMSO.

Crawley, H. (2010) *Chance or Choice? Understanding why asylum seekers come to the UK*, Refugee Council. Available from: www.refugeecouncil.org.uk/Resources/Refugee%20Council/downloads/rcchance.pdf

Cumming-Bruce, N. (2008) 'World's refugee count in 2007 exceeded 11 million, UN says', *New York Times*, 18 June. Available from: www.nytimes.com/2008/06/18/world/18refugees.html?_r=3andoref=slogin

Curran, James P. (2011) *Media and Democracy*, London: Routledge.

Daily Mail (2011a) 'Huge aid appeal as drought hits Horn of Africa', 9 July.

Daily Mail (2011b) 'Asylum seekers human rights claim that cost £110,000 went on even after complaint was settled', Daily Mail Online, 10 July. Available from: www.dailymail.co.uk/news/article-2013112/Asylum-seekers-human-rights-claim-cost-110-000-went-complaint-settled.html

Daily Mail (2012) 'Terror threat to Britain from the Arab Spring: UK extremists travelling to Al Qaeda training camps says MI5 chief', Daily Mail Online, 26 June. Available from: www.dailymail.co.uk/news/article-2164679/Terror-threat-Britain-Arab-Spring-UK-extremists-travelling-Al-Qaeda-training-camps-says-MI5-chief.html

Daniel, E. Valentine (ed.) (1995) *Mistrusting Refugees*, Berkeley, Calif.: University of California Press.

Davidson, D. (2008) 'Sky hands back Home Office payment for AFP series', brandrepublic.com, 15 September. Available from: www.brandrepublic.com/news/845936/Sky-hands-back-Home-Office-payment-AFP-series/

Dawn.com (2012) 'UN report predicts rise in world's displaced', Dawn.com, 1 June. Available from: http://dawn.com/2012/06/01/un-report-predicts-increase-in-worlds-displaced/

Der Spiegel (2007) 'Displaced on the rise: Iraq conflict fuels increase in refugees', 19 June. Available from: www.spiegel.de/international/world/displaced-on-the-rise-iraq-conflict-fuels-increase-in-refugees-a-489453.html

Eaton, G. (2011) 'What the anti-immigration lobby doesn't tell you', *New Statesman*, 1 November. Available from: www.newstatesman.com/blogs/the-staggers/2011/11/immigration-population-million

End of the Line (2009) Documentary, available on http://endoftheline.com/ (accessed 19 April 2013).

Express (2005) 'Bombers are all sponging asylum seekers', 27 July, p. 1.

Faculty of Public Health (2008) *The Health Needs of Asylum Seekers*, Available from: www.fph.org.uk/uploads/bs_aslym_seeker_health.pdf

Finney, N. (2003) *Asylum Seeker Dispersal: Public attitudes and press portrayals around the UK*, PhD thesis, Swansea: University of Wales.

Finney, N. (2005) *Key Issues: Public opinion on asylum and refugee issues,* Information Centre about Asylum and Refugees (ICAR). Available from: www.icar.org.uk/ng_attitudes%202005-10-19.pdf

Finney, N. and Peach, E. (2005) 'Attitudes towards asylum seekers, refugees and other immigrants', Commission for Racial Equality (CRE). Available from: www.icar.org.uk/asylum_icar_report.pdf

Gibney, M. (2008) 'Asylum and the expansion of deportation in the United Kingdom', *Government and Opposition*, vol. 43, no. 2, pp. 146–67.

Goodwin, Karen (2012) Speech by Refugee Council media officer at Developing Diversity in Scottish Media seminar organized by the Coalition for Racial Equality and Rights (CRER) and National Union of Journalists (NUJ), Glasgow, 11 October.

Greenslade, Roy (2005) 'Seeking scapegoats: the coverage of asylum in the press', working paper, London: Institute for Public Policy Research (IPPR).

Gross, B., Moore, K. and Threadgold, T. (2007) *Broadcast News Coverage of Asylum April to October 2006: Caught between human rights and public safety*, Cardiff: Cardiff School of Journalism, Media and Cultural Studies.

Guardian (2002a) 'Row erupts over Blunkett's "swamped" comment', 24 April. Available from: www.guardian.co.uk/politics/2002/apr/24/immigrationpolicy.immigrationandpublicservices

Guardian (2002b) 'Sangatte refugee camp', 23 May. Available from: www.guardian.co.uk/uk/2002/may/23/immigration.immigrationandpublicservices1

Guardian (2003) 'Blair predicts 50% drop in asylum seekers', 7 February. Available from: www.guardian.co.uk/politics/2003/feb/07/immigrationpolicy.immigration

Guardian (2005) 'Britain's strength lies in diversity', 5 August. Available from: www.guardian.co.uk/uk/2005/aug/05/britishidentity.july7

Guardian (2006a) 'PM defends asylum policy', 14 March. Available from: www.guardian.co.uk/politics/2006/mar/14/immigrationpolicy.immigrationandpublicservices

Guardian (2006b) 'Revolt brews over Australian Immigration Bill', 10 August. Available from: www.guardian.co.uk/world/2006/aug/10/australia.mainsection

Guardian (2007) 'Australia and US to swap refugees', 19 April. Available from: www.guardian.co.uk/world/2007/apr/19/australia.usa

Guardian (2009a) 'UK Borders Act 2007', 19 January. Available from: www.guardian.co.uk/commentisfree/libertycentral/2008/dec/16/uk-borders-act

Guardian (2009b) 'Borders, Citizenship and Immigration Act', 20 January. Available from: www.guardian.co.uk/commentisfree/libertycentral/2009/feb/13/civil-liberties-immigration

Guardian (2011a) 'UNHCR report says refugee numbers at 15-year high', 20 June. Available from: www.guardian.co.uk/world/2011/jun/20/unhcr-report-refugee-numbers-15-year-high

Guardian (2011b) 'Famine we could avoid: to pin the Somalia crisis on drought is wrong. This is an entirely predictable, man-made calamity', 22 July, p. 35.

Guardian (2011c) 'Taking deportation 'reserves' to airport condemned as inhumane', 26 July, p. 9.

Guardian (2011d) 'The more successful I got...', 27 July, p. 4.

Guardian (2011e) 'Comment: no refuge for refugees: despite Clegg's promises, child detention never quite went away, and is now making a comeback', 28 July, p. 30.

Guardian (2011f) 'EU agriculture policy "still hurting farmers in developing countries"', 11 October. Available from: www.guardian.co.uk/global-development/poverty-matters/2011/oct/11/eu-agriculture-hurts-developing-countries

Guardian (2012a) 'Abu Qatada deportation appeal rejected by human rights court', May 9. Available from: www.guardian.co.uk/world/2012/may/09/abu-qatada-deportation-appeal-rejected

Guardian (2012b) 'Academic refugees: "My hope is to contribute to this country – if I'm given the opportunity"', 31 August. Available from: www.guardian.co.uk/higher-education-network/blog/2012/aug/31/academic-refugees-latefa-guemar

Guardian (2012c) 'Double death in asylum seeker family reveals gap in state benefits', 5 October. Available from: www.guardian.co.uk/uk/2012/oct/05/immigration-children

Guardian (2012d) '"Unacceptable force" used by G4S staff deporting pregnant woman', 23 October. Available from: www.guardian.co.uk/uk/2012/oct/23/g4s-deportation-force-pregnant-woman

Gunder Frank, A. (1966) 'The development of under-development', in S. Corbridge (ed.), *Development Studies: A reader*, London: Arnold.

Hall, S., Critcher, C., Jefferson, T., Clarke, J. and Roberts, B. (1978) *Policing the Crisis: Mugging, the state and law and order*, London: Macmillan.

Hampshire, J. and Saggar, S. (2006) 'Migration, integration, and security in the UK since July 7', Migration Information.org, March. Available from: www.migrationinformation.org/USFocus/display.cfm?ID=383

Hansard (2010) 'Foreign national prisoners', 22 June. Available from: www.publications.parliament.uk/pa/cm201011/cmhansrd/cm100622/halltext/100622h0009.htm

Hartman, P. and Husband, C. (1974) *Racism and the Mass Media*, London: Davis-Poynter.

Hauser, M. (2000) *Chronology of chances in policy and practice affecting asylum seekers in the UK, 1992–1999*. Oxford: Refugee Studies Centre, University of Oxford.

Hayes, K. and Burge, R. (2003) *Coltan Mining in the Democratic Republic of Congo: How tantalum-using industries can commit to the reconstruction of the DRC*, Cambridge: Fauna and Flora International.

Home Office (1998) *Fairer, Faster and Firmer: A modern approach to immigration and asylum*. Available from: www.archive.official-documents. co.uk/document/cm40/4018/4018.htm

Home Office (2005a) *Asylum Statistics: 3rd quarter 2005*, London: Home Office.

Home Office (2005b) *Controlling Our Borders: Making migration work for Britain*. Available from: www.archive2.official-documents.co.uk/ document/cm64/6472/6472.pdf

Home Office (2007) *The Economic and Fiscal Impact of Immigration*, DWP, October. Available from: www.official-documents.gov.uk/document/ cm72/7237/7237.pdf

Hope, C. and Blake, H. (2011) 'WikiLeaks: Whitehall ignored warnings about "Londonistan" danger', *Telegraph,* 26 April. Available from: www. telegraph.co.uk/news/worldnews/wikileaks/8475556/WikiLeaks-White-hall-ignored-warnings-about-Londonistan-danger.html#

Hoselitz, Bert F. (1952) *The Progress of Underdeveloped Areas*, Chicago, Ill.: University of Chicago Press.

House of Commons (2006) *Select Committee on Home Affairs – 5th Report*, 15 July. Available from: www.publications.parliament.uk/pa/cm200506/ cmselect/cmhaff/775/77511.htm

House of Lords (2006) *The Human Rights Act: The DCA and Home Office reviews*, 7 November. Available from: www.publications.parliament.uk/ pa/jt200506/jtselect/jtrights/278/278.pdf

House of Lords (2008) *First Report of Select Committee on Economic Affairs*, 18 March. Available from: www.publications.parliament.uk/pa/ld200708/ ldselect/ldeconaf/82/8205.htm

Hyland, J. (1999) 'European governments turn against asylum seekers', World Socialist Web Site, 3 September. Available from: www.wsws.org/ articles/1999/sep1999/asyl-s03.shtml

Information Centre about Asylum and Refugees (ICAR) (2005) 'Reflecting asylum in London's communities'. Available from: www.icar.org.uk/ bob_html/02_gla_report/Reflecting_Asylum_Report.pdf

ICAR (2011) 'ICAR focus on March 2011: Ex foreign national offenders', 29 March. Available from: www.icar.org.uk/13133/icar-asylum-update/icar-focus-on-march-2011-ex-foreign-national-offenders.html

ICAR (2012) 'ICAR briefing: asylum seekers, refugees and media', February. Available from: www.icar.org.uk/Asylum_Seekers_and_Media_Briefing_ ICAR.pdf

Independent (2006) '"Soft targets" picked on for deportation, say refugee campaigners', 18 May. Available from: www.independent.co.uk/news/ uk/this-britain/soft-targets-picked-on-for-deportation-say-refugee-cam-paigners-478629.html

Independent (2011) 'Arab Spring refugees not welcome here, says William

Hague', 23 May. Available from: www.independent.co.uk/news/uk/politics/arab-spring-refugees-not-welcome-here-says-william-hague-2287795.html.

International Association for the study of Forced Migration (IAFM) (nd) http://iasfm.org/

Joint Committee on Human Rights (JCHR) (2007) *The Treatment of Asylum Seekers, Tenth report of session 2006–2007, Vol. 1*, London: HMSO.

Jones, S. (2010) 'ICAR population guide: Afghans in the UK', *ICAR*, July. Available from: www.icar.org.uk/Afghans%20in%20the%20UK.pdf

Kendall, P. and Wolf, K. (1949) 'The analysis of deviant case studies in communications research', in P. Lazarsfeld and F. Stanton (eds), *Communications Research 1948–1949*, New York: Harper.

'Killer Coke' campaign (nd) http://killercoke.org/crimes_mexico.php

Leveson, Lord Justice (2012) An Enquiry into the Culture, Practices and Ethics of the Press, November. Available at: www.official-documents.gov.uk/document/hc1213/hc07/0780/0780_ii.pdf

Lewis, M. (2005) *Asylum: Understanding public attitudes*, London: IPPR. Available from: www.ippr.org.uk/research/teams/project.asp?id=1576andpid=1576

McLaughlin, G. (1999) 'Refugees, migrants and the fall of the Berlin Wall', pp.197–210 in G. Philo (ed.), *Message Received*, Harlow: Longman.

Medic, N. (2004) 'How I took on the *Sun* – and lost', *Telegraph*, 15 July. Available from: www.telegraph.co.uk/news/uknews/1467073/How-I-took-on-The-Sun-and-lost.html

Mehmet, O. (1999) *Westernizing the Third World: The eurocentricity of economic development*, London: Routledge.

Migration Observatory (2011) *Thinking Behind the Numbers: Understanding public opinion on immigration in Britain*. Available from: http://migrationobservatory.ox.ac.uk/sites/files/migobs/Report%20-%20Public%20Opinion.pdf

Milne, S. and Travis, A. (2002) 'Blair's secret plan to crack down on asylum seekers' in *The Guardian*, 23 May. Available from:www.guardian.co.uk/uk/2002/may/23/immigration.immigrationandpublicservices2

Mirror (Eire) (2006) 'Hunger strike row stand-off; government adamant on asylum plea', 17 May, p. 2.

Mirror (UK) (2011) 'Camps can't handle the millions hit by drought', 11 July, p. 7.

Mirror (UK) (2011) 'My 3 year old was the first in our group to die ...', 12 July, pp. 22–3.

National Union of Journalists (2005) 'Fair play: refugees and asylum seekers in Scotland: a guide for journalists', Scotland: Oxfam.

Observer (2006) Leader, 14 May.

Oxfam (2007) 'Global trends', *Evolution* 7. Available from: www.evolution7.com.au/archive/oxfam/global-trends-statistics.html

Pallister, David (2007) 'The numbers game', *Guardian*, 21 March. Available from: www.guardian.co.uk/commentisfree/2007/mar/21/themarsbarhasa

PBS (2008) 'Indian farmers, Coca-Cola vie for scarce water supply', 17 November. Available from: www.pbs.org/newshour/bb/asia/july-dec08/waterwars_11-17.html (accessed 26 April 2013).

Perkins, Richard and Neumayer, Eric (2010) 'The organized hypocrisy of ethical foreign policy: human rights, democracy and Western arms sales', *Geoforum*, vol. 41, no. 2, pp. 247–56.

Philo, G. (1990) *Seeing and Believing: The influence of television*, London: Routledge.

Philo, G. and Beattie, L. (1999) 'Race, migration and media', pp.171–96 in G. Philo (ed.), *Message Received*, Harlow: Longman,.

Philo, G. and Berry, M. (2011) *Bad News for Israel*, London: Pluto Press.

Philo, G., Hilsum, L., Beattie, L. and Holliman, R. (1998) 'The media and the Rwandan crisis: effects on audiences and public policy', in J. W. Pieterse (ed.), *World Orders in the Making*, London: Macmillan.

Powerbase (2007) *Migration Watch*. Available from: www.powerbase.info/index.php/MigrationWatch#cite_note-3

Press Association (2006) 'Yesterday in Parliament', *Guardian*, 16 May. Available from: www.guardian.co.uk/politics/2006/may/16/houseofcommons

Prince, R. (2010) 'How Tony Blair's 12 point anti-terror plan after 7/7 came to little', *Telegraph*, 1 January. Available from: www.telegraph.co.uk/news/uknews/terrorism-in-the-uk/6921374/How-Tony-Blairs-12-point-anti-terror-plan-after-77-came-to-little.html

Quakers Asylum and Refugee Network (2012) 'Lord Ramsbotham, former chief inspector of prisons, attacks "perverse" decision not to prosecute G4S over Mubenga death', 20 July. Available from: www.qarn.org.uk/homepage/lord-ramsbotham-former-chief-inspector-of-prisons-attacks-perverse-decision-not-to-prosecute-g4s-over-mubenga-death/

Refugee Action (2006) *The Destitution Trap*. Available from: www.refugee-action.org.uk/campaigns/documents/RA_DestReport_Final_LR.pdf

Refugee Action (2012) 'Information', Refugee Action Online. Available from: www.refugee-action.org.uk/information/asylumandterrorism.aspx

Refugee Council (2010a) *Employing Refugees: A guide for employers*. Available from: www.equalityhumanrights.com/uploaded_files/employing_refugees_guide.pdf

Refugee Council (2010b) 'Refugee Council response to first quarterly asylum statistics for 2010', Refugee Council Online, 28 May. Available from: www.refugeecouncil.org.uk/news/archive/press/2010/may/20100528_b

Refugee Council (2012) 'Security firms awarded contracts for housing asylum seekers: our response', *Refugee Council Online*, 23 March. Available from: www.refugeecouncil.org.uk/latest/news/771_security_firms_awarded_contracts_for_housing_asylum_seekers_our_response

Refugee Council (2013) *Brief Guide to Asylum*, February. Available from: www.refugeecouncil.org.uk/assets/0002/5610/Asylum_Briefing_2013.pdf

Reubner, J. (2011) 'Disincentives to peace: US weapons sales to Israel', *Counterpunch*, 22 April. Available from: http://www.informationclearinghouse.info/article27947.htm

Revill, J. and Doward, J. (2007). 'BNP backs Hodge in housing row', *Observer*, 27 May. Available from: www.guardian.co.uk/politics/2007/may/27/thefarright.communities

Reynolds, S. and Muggeridge, H. (2008) 'Remote controls: how UK border controls are endangering the lives of refugees', Refugee Council Online. Available from: www.refugeecouncil.org.uk/Resources/Refugee%20Council/downloads/researchreports/Remote%20Controls.pdf

Roberts, D. (2006) 'A mockery of the immigration system', *Telegraph*, 17 May. Available from: www.telegraph.co.uk/news/uknews/1518561/A-mockery-of-the-immigration-system.html

Robinson, D. (2009) 'New immigrants and migrants in social housing in Britain: discursive themes and lived realities', Policy Press. Available from: http://learning.chs.ac.uk/file.php/1/New_immigrants-_Migrants_in_socia_housing_in_Britain.pdf

Robinson, V. and Segrott, J. (2002) *Understanding the Decision Making of Asylum Seekers*, Research Study 243, London: Home Office.

Rogers, S. (2012) 'British Social Attitudes Survey – how what we think and who thinks it has changed', *Guardian*, 17 September. Available from: www.guardian.co.uk/news/datablog/2012/sep/17/british-social-attitudes-historic-data

Rostow, W. W. (1960) *The Stages of Economic Growth: A non-communist manifesto*, Cambridge: Cambridge University Press.

Ryan, M (2003) 'Blunkett "fuelled" asylum fears', BBC Online, 23 January. Available from: http://news.bbc.co.uk/1/hi/uk_politics/2688023.stm

Sahn, D., Dorosh, P. and Younger, S. (1997) *Structural Adjustment Reconsidered: Economic policy and poverty in Africa*, Cambridge: Cambridge University Press.

Said, E. (1978) *Orientalism: Western conceptions of the Orient*, London: Routledge & Kegan Paul.

Scottish Refugee Council (2012) 'Scottish Daily Mail apologises for misleading story about legal bids for asylum seekers', Scottish Refugee Council Online, 1 March Available from: www.scottishrefugeecouncil.org.uk/news_and_events/latest_news/1518_scottish_daily_mail_apologises_for_misleading_story_about_legal_bids_for_asylum_seekers

Scottish Sun (2011) '£80m benefits spree for asylum seekers', 11 November. Available from: www.thescottishsun.co.uk/scotsol/homepage/news/3908738/80m-benefits-spree-for-asylum-seekers.html

Sun (2011a) 'This is an epic crisis far worse than one which led to Band Aid; Refugee camp swamped by thousands after drought', 11 July, pp. 30–1.

Sun (2011b) '£110k asylum rap', 11 July, p. 13.

Sun (2011c) 'We haven't lost a child for 12 days but starving and sick keep pouring in', 12 July, p. 20.

Teather, S. (2013) *Report of the Parliamentary Inquiry into Asylum support for Children and Young People*, January. Available from: www.childrenssociety.org.uk/sites/default/files/tcs/asylum_support_inquiry_report_final.pdf

Temko, N. and Doward, J. (2006) 'Revealed – Blair attack on Human Rights Law', *Guardian*, 14 May. Available from: www.guardian.co.uk/politics/2006/may/14/humanrights.ukcrime

Thompson, T. (2003) 'Asylum seekers and crime', *Guardian*, 25 May. Available from: www.guardian.co.uk/politics/2003/may/25/immigration.race

Today (2009) 'UK "seen as soft touch" on immigration', BBC Radio 4, 19 September.

United Nations (2012) 'Refugees' in *Resources for Speakers on Global Issues*. Available from: www.un.org/en/globalissues/briefingpapers/refugees/nextsteps.html

UN High Commissioner for Refugees (UNHCR) (1951/1967) 'Convention and Protocol Relating to the Status of Refugees', in *Refugee Action*. Available from: www.refugee-action.org.uk/information/documents/convention.pdf

UNHCR (2002) 'The world of refugee women at a glance', *Refugee Magazine*, no. 126, Available from: www.unhcr.org/3cb5508b2.html

UNHCR (2005) *Quality Initiative Project: Second report to the Minister*, London: UNHCR.

UNHCR (2007) *Information and Briefings to The Conservative Party National and International Security Policy Group*, March. Available from: www.unhcr.org.uk/fileadmin/user_upload/pdf/Information_and_briefings2.pdf

UNHCR (2008) Response to Home Office Border Agency consultation, 'The Path to Citizenship: Next Steps in Reforming the Immigration System'. Available from: www.unhcr.org.uk/fileadmin/user_upload/pdf/080516ResponsetoHomeOfficeBorderAgencyconsultationoncitizenship.pdf

UNHCR (2011) *Global Trends 2011 Report*. Available from: www.unhcr.org/4fd6f87f9.html

US Congress (2002) 'HR4775' Supplemental Appropriations Act 2002. Available from: www.govtrack.us/congress/bills/107/hr4775/text

Van Dijk, T. C. (1991) *Racism and the Press*, London: Routledge.

Van Steenburgen, M. (2012) 'Third detainee threatens to jump from detention centre rooftop', *Guardian – The Northerner Blog*, 15 August. Available from: www.guardian.co.uk/uk/the-northerner/2012/aug/15/immigration-refugees-asylum-morton-hall-protest

Vargas, Jose Antonio (2011) 'Jose reports: view from somewhere – a real conversation on immigration,' *Define America*, 27 September.

Verkaik, R. (2006) 'UN criticises Home Office over refugees', *Independent*, 28 June. Available from: www.independent.co.uk/news/uk/politics/un-criticises-home-office-over-refugees-405762.html

Walt, Stephen (2012) *Foreign Policy*. Available from: http://walt.foreignpolicy.com/

Waltz, Kenneth Neal (1979) *Theory of International Politics*, Boston, Mass./London: McGraw-Hill.

Webber, F. (2011) 'A mighty victory for FNPs', IRR, 24 March. Available from: www.irr.org.uk/news/a-mighty-victory-for-fnps/

Welch, M. and Schuster, L. (2005) 'Detention of asylum seekers in the UK and the USA: deciphering noisy and quiet constructions', *Punishment Society*, no. 7, pp. 397–417.

Williams, Zoe (2013) 'For failed asylum seekers, life on Section 4 is a nightmare worse than Kafka', *Guardian*, 30 January. Available from: www.guardian.co.uk/commentisfree/2013/jan/30/asylum-theresa-may-private-fiefdom

Index

MAKING PEACE WITH THE EARTH
Vandana Shiva

'Shiva is one of the world's most prominent radical scientists.'
– *Guardian*

Vandana Shiva takes the reader on a journey through the
world's devastated eco-landscape, one of genetic engineering,
industrial development and land-grabs in Africa, Asia and
South America. The book outlines how a paradigm shift to
earth-centred politics and economics is our only chance of
survival and how collective resistance to corporate exploitation
can open the way to a new environmentalism.

SHADOW LIVES
The Forgotten Women of the War on Terror
Victoria Brittain
Foreword by John Berger

'A searching, sensitive account of the ordeal of the women
left behind, their torment, their endurance and courage,
their triumphs over the cruel "extension of prison to home."
And not least, a revealing picture of what we have allowed
ourselves to become.' – *Noam Chomsky*

Shadow Lives reveals the unseen side of the '9/11 wars': their
impact on the wives and families of men incarcerated in
Guantanamo, or in prison or under house arrest.

PlutoPress
www.plutobooks.com

GENERATION PALESTINE
Voices from the Boycott, Divestment and Sanctions Movement
Edited by Rich Wiles
Foreword by Archbishop Desmond Tutu

'The BDS movement is the most enlightened, imaginative, moral, fearless and dynamic blow for freedom I have known for many years. I believe it will be a vital factor in the liberation of Palestine. The inspiring voices in this book will help achieve that goal.' – *John Pilger*

Contributors include Ken Loach, Iain Banks, Ronnie Kasrils, Professor Richard Falk, Ilan Pappe, Omar Barghouti, Ramzy Baroud and Archbishop Attallah Hannah, alongside other internationally acclaimed artists, writers, academics and grassroots activists.

IT'S THE POLITICAL ECONOMY, STUPID
The Global Financial Crisis in Art and Theory
Edited by Gregory Sholette and Oliver Ressler

It's the Political Economy, Stupid brings together internationally acclaimed artists and thinkers, including Slavoj Žižek, David Graeber, Judith Butler and Brian Holmes, to focus on the current economic crisis. By combining artistic responses with the analysis of leading radical theorists, the book expands the boundaries of critique beyond the usual discourse.

 PlutoPress
www.plutobooks.com

MURDOCH'S POLITICS
*How One Man's Thirst For Wealth and Power
Shapes our World*
David McKnight
Foreword by Robert W. McChesney

'An anatomy and record of the reign of Murdoch which is
brave and valuable. One day, when Murdoch is gone, it will
help explain why so many obeyed him.' – *Guardian*

When Rupert Murdoch called, prime ministers and presidents
picked up the phone. David McKnight exposes Murdoch's
unflinching use of his media empire to further his political
agenda over decades. This is the story behind the hacking
scandal that rocked the word and shook the Murdoch empire.

POWER BEYOND SCRUTINY
Media, Justice and Accountability
Justin Schlosberg

'This is a book by one of the new generation's rising stars
that examines the forces that limit investigative journalism.' –
Professor James Curran, Goldsmiths, University of London

Power Beyond Scrutiny uncovers the forces which distort and limit
public debate in the media. Schlosberg shows how news silences
are more than just accidents. They are ideological forces which
ensure that dissent remains within definable limits.

PlutoPress
www.plutobooks.com

THE HERETIC'S GUIDE TO GLOBAL FINANCE
Hacking the Future of Money
Brett Scott

'A unique inside-out look at our financial system. It is not only a user-friendly guide to the complex maze of modern finance but also a manual for utilising and subverting it for social purposes in innovative ways. Smart and street-smart.' – *Ha-Joon Chang*

'An imaginative, even exuberant exploration of the daunting world of finance – it will unleash a generation of activists, and do a world of good.' – *Bill McKibben*

HOW A CENTURY OF WAR CHANGED THE LIVES OF WOMEN
Lindsey German

'German tells a fascinating and important story.' – *Nina Power, author of* One-Dimensional Woman

Lindsey German, one of the UK's leading anti-war activists and commentators, shows how women have played a central role in anti-war and peace movements, including the recent wars in Afghanistan and Iraq. As well as providing an inspiring account of women's opposition to war, the book also tackles key contemporary developments, challenging negative assumptions about Muslim women and showing how anti-war movements are feeding into a broader desire to change society.

PlutoPress
www.plutobooks.com